C# Essentials

C# Essentials

Ben Albahari, Peter Drayton, and Brad Merrill

O'REILLY®

Beijing · Cambridge · Farnham · Köln · Paris · Sebastopol · Taipei · Tokyo

C# Essentials

by Ben Albahari, Peter Drayton, and Brad Merrill

Editor: John Osborn

Production Editor: Mary Anne Weeks Mayo

Cover Designer: Ellie Volckhausen

Printing History:

      February 2001:   First Edition.

ISBN: 0-596-00079-0

[M]

Table of Contents

Preface

C# Essentials is a highly condensed introduction to the C# language and the .NET Framework. C# and the .NET initiative were both unveiled in July 2000 at the Microsoft Professional Developers Conference in Orlando, Florida, and shortly thereafter the .NET Software Development Kit (SDK) was released on the Internet.

The information in this book is based on the beta 1 version of the .NET SDK released by Microsoft in November 2000. We expect both the C# language and the .NET Framework to continue to evolve over the coming months. To stay current, be sure to check the online resources listed in the section "C# Online" as well as the O'Reilly web page for this book (see the section "How to Contact Us").

Audience

While we have tried to make this book useful to anyone interested in learning about C#, our primary audience is developers already familiar with an object-oriented language such as C++, Smalltalk, Java, or Delphi. C# facilitates writing web applications and services, as well as traditional standalone and client/server-based applications. Experience in any of these areas will make the advantages of C# and the .NET Framework more immediately apparent but isn't required.

About This Book

This book is divided into five chapters and six appendixes:

Chapter 1, *Introduction*, orients you to C# and the .NET Framework.

Chapter 2, *C# Language Reference*, introduces the C# language and also serves as a language reference.

Chapter 3, *Programming the .NET Framework*, explains how to use C# and the .NET Framework.

Chapter 4, *Base Class Library Overview*, provides an overview of the key libraries in .NET—organized by function—and documents the most essential namespaces and types of each.

Chapter 5, *Essential .NET Tools*, is an overview of essential .NET tools that ship with the .NET Framework SDK, including the C# compiler and utilities for importing COM objects and exporting .NET objects.

The six appendixes provide additional information of interest to working programmers, including an alphabetical C# keyword reference, codes for regular expressions and string formats, and a cross reference of assembly and namespace mappings

This book assumes that you have access to a beta version of the .NET Framework SDK. For additional details on language features and class libraries covered here, we recommend the Microsoft online .NET documentation.

C# Online

C# and the .NET Framework will continue to evolve over the coming months as Microsoft readies both for release. In addition, the submission of C# and the Common Language Infrastructure (CLI) to ECMA for standardization will inevitably lead to additional changes.

To stay up-to-date on the latest developments, you should periodically visit the O'Reilly web page (see the section "How to Contact Us").

We also recommend the following sites:

http://msdn.microsoft.com/net/
> The Microsoft .NET Developer Center is the official site for all things .NET, including the latest version of the .NET Framework SDK, which includes the C# compiler, as well as documentation, technical articles, sample code, pointers to discussion groups, and third-party resources.

http://msdn.microsoft.com/net/thirdparty/default.asp
> A complete list of third party resources of interest to C# and .NET
> Framework developers.

http://discuss.develop.com/dotnet.html
> The DevelopMentor DOTNET discussion list. Possibly the best site for
> free-wheeling independent discussion of the .NET languages and
> framework; participants often include key Microsoft engineers.

http://www.devx.com/dotnet/resources/
> The DevX listing of online .NET resources. Very comprehensive and
> thorough.

Two articles of interest include:

http://windows.oreilly.com/news/hejlsberg_0800.html
> An interview with chief C# architect Anders Hejlsberg, by O'Reilly
> editor John Osborn.

http://www.genamics.com/visualj++/csharp_comparative.htm
> A comparison of C# to C++ and Java, by coauthor Ben Albahari.

Conventions Used in This Book

Throughout this book we use these typographic conventions:

Italic
> Represents the names of system elements such as directories and files
> and Internet resources, such as URLs and web documents. Italics is
> also used for new terms when they are defined and, occasionally, for
> emphasis in body text.

`Constant width`
> Indicates language constructs such as .NET and application-defined
> types, namespaces, and functions, as well as keywords, constants, and
> expressions that should be typed verbatim. Lines of code and code
> fragments also appear in constant width, as do classes, class members,
> and XML tags.

`Constant width italic`
> Represents replaceable parameter names or user-provided elements in
> syntax.

We have included simple grammar specifications for many, but not all, of
the language constructs presented in this book. Our intent is not to be
comprehensive—for that level of detail you should consult the Microsoft
C# Language Reference in the .NET SDK—but rather to provide you with
a fast way to understand the grammar of a particular construct and its

valid combinations. The XML occurrence operators (?,*, and +) are used to specify more precisely the number of times an element may occur in a particular construct.

x   Indicates *x* is to be used verbatim (`constant width`).

x   Indicates *x* is supplied by the programmer (`constant width italic`).

x? Indicates *x* may occur zero-or-one times.

*x** Indicates *x* may occur zero-or-more times, separated by commas.

x+ Indicates *x* may occur one-or-more times, separated by commas.

[...]

Indicates a logical grouping of code elements, when not implicitly grouped using the verbatim terms {}, (), and [].

[x | y]

Indicates only one of a choice of code elements may occur.

The owl icon designates a note, which is an important aside to the nearby text.

The turkey icon designates a warning relating to the nearby text.

How to Contact Us

Please address comments and questions concerning this book to the publisher:

O'Reilly & Associates, Inc.
101 Morris Street
Sebastopol, CA 95472
(800) 998-9938 (in the United States or Canada)
(707) 829-0515 (international or local)
(707) 829-0104 (fax)

We have a web page for this book, where we list errata, examples, or any additional information. You can access this page at:

http://www.oreilly.com/catalog/csharpess

To comment or ask technical questions about this book, send email to:

bookquestions@oreilly.com

For more information about our books, conferences, software, Resource Centers, and the O'Reilly Network, see our web site at:

http://www.oreilly.com

Acknowledgments

This book would not be possible without the contribution and support of many individuals, including friends, family, and the hard-working folks at O'Reilly & Associates, Inc.

All three of us wish to thank Jeff Peil for his contributions to the sections of this book that deal with threads and interop. Many thanks as well to Scott Wiltamuth, Joe Nalewabu, Andrew McMullen, and Michael Perry, whose technical reviews have immeasurably improved our text.

Ben Albahari

First of all, I'd like to thank my family (Sonia, Miri, and Joseph Albahari) and friends (most of all Marcel Dinger and Lenny Geros) for still wanting to know me given that I'm practically epoxied to my computer. I'd also like to thank all the bands (can't list them all but particularly Fiona Apple, Dream Theater, and Incubus during this writing period) for the CDs that clutter my desk, without which I would never have been motivated enough to stay up to till 5:00 a.m. to simulate being in the same time zone as the great people in America I worked with when writing this book (John Osborn, Peter Drayton, and Brad Merrill). Finally I'd like to thank everyone who is enthusiastic about new technology, which ultimately is what drove me to write this book. I'd like to dedicate this book to my late father, Michael, to whom I am indebted for his foresight in introducing me to programming when I was a child.

Peter Drayton

Above all, I'd like to thank my wife, Julie DuBois, for her constant, loving support. Regardless of how engrossing the world of bits can be, you serve as a constant reminder of how much more wonderful the world of atoms really is. I'd like to thank my coauthors, Ben and Brad, for so graciously affording me the opportunity of participating in this project, and our editor, John Osborn, for keeping all three of us pointed in the same direction during the wild ride that resulted in this book. I'd also like to thank my friends and colleagues (most notably John Prout, Simon Fell, Simon Shortman, and Chris Torkildson) who serve as trusty sounding-boards on technical and life issues. Finally, I'd like to thank my family back in South Africa, especially my father, Peter Drayton Sr., and my late mother, Irene Mary Rochford Drayton, for giving me a strong rudder to navigate through life.

Brad Merrill

I'd like to thank my son Haeley, my partner Jodi, my coparent Cyprienne, and my friends (Larry, Colleen, and Evan) for their patience and support during this process. I'd also like to thank Ben and Peter for their immense contributions, and our editor John Osborn for keeping us sane.

1

Introduction

C# is a language built specifically to program the new Microsoft .NET Framework. The .NET Framework consists of a runtime environment called the Common Language Runtime (CLR), and a set of base class libraries, which provide a rich development platform that can be exploited by a variety of languages and tools.

C# Language

Programming languages have strengths in different areas. Some languages are powerful but can be bug-prone and difficult to work with, while others are simpler but can be limiting in terms of functionality or performance. C# is a new language designed to provide an optimum blend of simplicity, expressiveness, and performance.

Many features of C# were designed in response to the strengths and weaknesses of other languages, particularly Java and C++. The C# language specification was written by Anders Hejlsberg and Scott Wiltamuth. Anders Hejlsberg is famous in the programming world for creating the Turbo Pascal compiler and leading the team that designed Delphi.

Key features of the C# language include the following:

Component orientation

An excellent way to manage complexity in a program is to subdivide it into several interacting components, some of which can be used in multiple scenarios. C# has been designed to make component building easy and provides component-oriented language constructs such as properties, events, and declarative constructs called *attributes*.

One-stop coding

Everything pertaining to a declaration in C# is localized to the declaration itself, rather than being spread across several source files or several places within a source file. Types do not require additional declarations in separate header or Interface Definition Language (IDL) files, a property's get/set methods are logically grouped, documentation is embedded directly in a declaration, etc. Furthermore, because declaration order is irrelevant types don't require a separate stub declaration to be used by another type.

Versioning

C# provides features such as explicit interface implementations, hiding inherited members, and read-only modifiers, which help new versions of a component work with older components that depend on it.

Safe type system

C# is *type-safe*, which ensures that a variable can be accessed only through the type associated with that variable. This encapsulation encourages good programming design and eliminates potential bugs or security breaches by making it impossible for one variable to inadvertently or maliciously overwrite another.

All C# types (including primitive types) derive from a single base type, providing a *unified type system*. This means all types—structs, interfaces, delegates, enums, and arrays—share the same basic functionality, such as the ability to be converted to a string, serialized, or stored in a collection.

Automatic memory management

C# relies on a runtime that performs automatic memory management. This frees programmers from disposing objects, which eliminates problems such as dangling pointers, memory leaks, and coping with circular references.

However, C# does not eliminate pointers: it merely makes them unnecessary for most programming tasks. For performance-critical hotspots and interoperability, pointers may be used, but they are only permitted in unsafe blocks that require a high security permission to execute.

Leveraging of the CLR

A big advantage of C# over other languages, particularly traditionally compiled languages such as C++, is its close fit with the .NET CLR. Many aspects of C# alias the CLR, especially its type system, memory-management model, and exception-handling mechanism.

Common Language Runtime

Of fundamental importance to the .NET framework is the fact that programs are executed within a managed execution environment provided by the Common Language Runtime. The CLR greatly improves runtime interactivity between programs, portability, security, development simplicity, cross-language integration, and provides an excellent foundation for a rich set of class libraries.

Absolutely key to these benefits is the way .NET programs are compiled. Each language targeting .NET compiles source code and produces *metadata* and Microsoft Intermediate Language (MSIL) code. Metadata includes a complete specification for a program including all its types, apart from the actual implementation of each function. These implementations are stored as MSIL, which is machine-independent code that describes the instructions of a program. The CLR uses this "blueprint" to bring a .NET program to life at runtime, providing services far beyond what is possible with the traditional approach—compiling code directly to assembly language.

Key features of the CLR include the following:

Runtime interactivity

Programs can richly interact with each other at runtime through their metadata. A program can search for new types at runtime, then instantiate and invoke methods on those types.

Portability

Programs can be run without recompiling on any operating system and processor combination that supports the CLR. A key element of this platform independence is the runtime's JIT (Just-In-Time Compiler), which compiles the MSIL code it is fed to native code that runs on the underlying platform.

Security

Security considerations permeate the design of the .NET Framework. Key to making this possible is CLR's ability to analyze MSIL instructions as being safe or unsafe.

Simplified deployment

An *assembly* is a completely self-describing package that contains all the metadata and MSIL of a program. Deployment can be as easy as copying the assembly to the client computer.

Versioning

An assembly can function properly with new versions of assemblies it depends on without recompilation. Key to making this possible is the ability to resolve all type references though metadata.

Simplified development

The CLR provides many features that greatly simplify development, including services such as garbage collection, exception handling, debugging, and profiling.

Cross language integration

The Common Type System (CTS) of the CLR defines the types that can be expressed in metadata and MSIL and the possible operations that can be performed on those types. The CTS is broad enough to support many different languages, including Microsoft languages, such as C#, VB.NET, and VC.NET, and such third party languages as COBOL, Eiffel, Haskell, Mercury, ML, Oberon, Perl, Python, Smalltalk, and Scheme.

The Common Language Specification (CLS) defines a subset of the CTS, which provides a common standard that enables .NET languages to share and extend each other's libraries. For instance, an Eiffel programmer can create a class that derives from a C# class and override its virtual methods.

Interoperability with legacy code

The CLR provides interoperation with the vast base of existing software written in COM and C. .NET types can be exposed as COM types, and COM types can be imported as .NET types. In addition, the CLR provides PInvoke, which is a mechanism that enables C functions, structs, and callbacks to be easily used from within in a .NET program.

Base Class Libraries

The .NET Framework provides the Base Class Libraries (BCL), which can be used by all languages. These libraries range from those that are a portal to core functionality of the runtime, such as threading and runtime manipulation of types (reflection), to libraries that provide high-level functionality, such as data access, rich client support, and web services (whereby code can even be embedded in a web page). C# has almost no built-in libraries; it uses the BCL instead.

A Minimal C# Program

A minimal C# program is implemented like this:

```
class Test {
    static void Main() {
        System.Console.WriteLine("Welcome to C#!");
    }
}
```

All C# statements are scoped to methods (or special forms of methods), and all methods are scoped to types, such as the class Test. The Main method is recognized as the default entry point of execution, static means the method is an ordinary procedure that does not require an instance of Test to execute, and void means the method does not return a value. System is a namespace containing many related types, one of which is Console. Console is the class that encapsulates standard input/output functionality and has many methods including WriteLine. The brackets, braces, and semicolons are necessary to group and state things unambiguously, and the indentation is there for readability.

To compile this program into an executable, paste it into a text file, save it as *Test.cs*, then type cs Test.cs in the command prompt. This compiles the program into an executable called *Test.exe*.

2

C# Language Reference

This chapter walks you through each aspect of the C# language. Many features of C# will be familiar if you have experience with a strongly typed object-oriented language.

Identifiers

Identifiers are names programmers choose for their types, methods, variables, and so on. An identifier must be a whole word, essentially composed of Unicode characters starting with a letter or underscore. An identifier must not clash with a keyword. As a special case, the @ prefix can be used to avoid such a conflict, but the character isn't considered part of the identifier that it precedes. For instance, the following two identifiers are equivalent:

```
KoЯn
@KoЯn
```

C# identifiers are case-sensitive, but for compatibility with other languages, you should not differentiate public or protected identifiers by case alone.

Types

A C# program is written by building new *types* and leveraging existing types, either those defined in the C# language itself or imported from other libraries. Each type contains a set of data and function members, which combine to form the modular units that are the key building blocks of a C# program.

Type Instances

Generally, you must create instances of a type to use that type. Those data members and function members that require a type to be *instantiated* are called *instance members*. Data members and function members that can be used on the type itself are called *static members*.

Example: Building and Using Types

In this program, we build our own type called `Counter` and another type called `Test` that uses instances of the `Counter`. The `Counter` type uses the predefined type `int`, and the `Test` type uses the static function member `WriteLine` of the `Console` class defined in the `System` namespace:

```
// Imports types from System namespace, such as Console
using System;
class Counter { // New types are typically classes or structs
  // --- Data members ---
  int value; // field of type int
  int scaleFactor; // field of type int

  // Constructor, used to initialize a type instance
  public Counter(int scaleFactor) {
    this.scaleFactor = scaleFactor;
  }
  // Method
  public void Inc() {
    value+=scaleFactor;
  }
  // Property
  public int Count {
    get {return value; }
  }
}
class Test {
  // Execution begins here
  static void Main() {

    // Create an instance of counter type
    Counter c = new Counter(5);
    c.Inc();
    c.Inc();
    Console.WriteLine(c.Count); // prints "10";

    // Create another instance of counter type
    Counter d = new Counter(7);
    d.Inc();
```

```
    Console.WriteLine(d.Count); // prints "7";
  }
}
```

Implicit and Explicit Conversions

Each type has its own set of rules defining how it can be converted to and from other types. Conversions between types may be implicit or explicit. *Implicit* conversions can be performed automatically, while *explicit* conversions require a *cast* using the C cast operator, ().

```
int x = 123456; // int is a 4-byte integer
long y = x; // implicit conversion to 8-byte integer
short z =(short)x // explicit conversion to 2-byte integer
```

Implicit conversions are guaranteed to succeed and not lose information. Conversely, an explicit conversion is required when runtime circumstances determine whether the conversion succeeds or when information might be lost during the conversion.

Most conversion rules are supplied by the language, such as the previous numeric conversions. Occasionally it is useful for developers to define their own implicit and explicit conversions (see the section "Expressions and Operators").

Categories of Types

All C# types, including both predefined types and user-defined types, fall into one of three categories: *value, reference,* and *pointer.*

Value types

Value types typically represent basic types. Simple types, such as basic numeric types (int, long, bool, etc.) are structs, which are value types. You can expand the set of simple types by defining your own structs. In addition, C# allows you to define enums.

Reference types

Reference types typically represent more complex types with rich functionality. The most fundamental C# reference type is the class, but special functionality is provided by the array, delegate, and interface types.

Pointer types

Pointer types fall outside mainstream C# usage and are used only for explicit memory manipulation in unsafe blocks (see the section "Unsafe Code and Pointers").

Predefined Types

C# has two categories of predefined types:

- Value types: integers, floating point numbers, decimal, char, bool
- Reference types: object, string

All these alias types can be found in the System namespace. For example, the following two statements are semantically identical:

```
int i = 5;
System.Int32 i = 5;
```

Integral types

The following table describes integral types:

C# Type	System Type	Size (bytes)	Signed?
sbyte	System.Sbyte	1	Yes
short	System.Int16	2	Yes
int	System.Int32	4	Yes
long	System.Int64	8	Yes
byte	System.Byte	1	No
ushort	System.UInt16	2	No
uint	System.UInt32	4	No
ulong	System.UInt64	8	No

sbyte, short, int, and long are signed integers; byte, ushort, uint, and ulong are unsigned integers.

For unsigned integers n bits wide, their possible values range from 0 to 2^n-1. For signed integers n bits wide, their possible values range from -2^{n-1} to $2^{n-1}-1$. Integer literals can use either decimal or hexadecimal notation:

```
int x = 5;
ulong y = 0x1234AF; // prefix with 0x for hexadecimal
```

When an integral literal is valid for several possible integral types, the default type chosen goes in this order:

```
int
uint
long
ulong.
```

These suffixes may be appended to a value to explicitly specify its type:

U   `uint` or `ulong`

L   `long` or `ulong`

UL `ulong`

Integral conversions. An implicit conversion between integral types is permitted when the type to convert to contains every possible value of the type to convert from. Otherwise an explicit conversion is required. For instance, you can implicitly convert an `int` to a `long`, but must explicitly convert an `int` to a `short`:

```
int x = 123456;
long y = x; // implicit, no information lost
short z = (short)x; // explicit, truncates x
```

Floating-point types

C# Type	System Type	Size (bytes)
float	System.Single	4
double	System.Double	8

A `float` can hold values from approximately $\pm1.5 \times 10^{-45}$ to approximately $\pm3.4 \times 10^{38}$ with 7 significant figures.

A `double` can hold values from approximately $\pm5.0 \times 10^{-324}$ to approximately $\pm1.7 \times 10^{308}$ with 15 to 16 significant figures.

Floating-point types can hold the special values +0, -0, +∞, -∞, or NaN (not a number) that represent the outcome of mathematical operations such as division by zero. `float` and `double` implement the specification of the IEEE 754 format types, supported by almost all processors, defined by *http://www.ieee.org.*

Floating-point literals can use decimal or exponential notation. A `float` literal requires the suffix "f" or "F". A `double` literal may choose to add the suffix "d" or "D".

```
float x = 9.81f;
double y = 7E-02; // 0.07
```

Floating-point conversions. An implicit conversion from a `float` to a `double` loses no information and is permitted but not vice versa. An implicit conversion from an `int`, `uint`, or `long` to a `float`, and from a `long` to a `double`, is allowed, for readability:

```
int strength = 2;
int offset = 3;
float x = 9.53f * strenngtgth - offset;
```

If this example used larger values, precision might be lost. However, the possible range of values isn't truncated, because the lowest and highest possible values of a **float** or **double** exceed those of an **int**, **unit**, or **long**'s lowest of highest value. All other conversions between integral and floating-point types must be explicit:

```
float x = 3.53f;
int offset = (int)x;
```

decimal type

C# Type	System Type	Size (bytes)
decimal	System.Decimal	12

The **decimal** type can hold values from $\pm 1.0 \times 10^{-28}$ to approximately $\pm 7.9 \times 10^{28}$ with 28 to 29 significant figures.

The **decimal** type holds 28 digits and the position of the decimal point on those digits. Unlike a floating-point value, it has more precision but a smaller range. It is typically useful in financial calculations, where the combination of its high precision and the ability to store a base$_{10}$ number without rounding errors is valuable. The number 0.1, for instance, is represented exactly with a **decimal**, but as a recurring binary number with a floating-point type. There is no concept of +0, -0, +∞, -∞, and NaN for a decimal.

A **decimal** literal requires the suffix "m" or "M":

```
decimal x = 80603.454327m; // holds exact value
```

decimal conversions. An implicit conversion from all integral types to a decimal type is permitted because a **decimal** type can represent every possible integer value. A conversion from a **decimal** to floating type or vice versa requires an explicit conversion, since floating-point types have a bigger range than a **decimal**, and a decimal has more precision than a floating-point type.

char type

C# Type	System Type	Size (bytes)
Char	System.Char	2

The **char** type represents a Unicode character.

A **char** literal consists of either a character, Unicode format, or escape
character enclosed in single quote marks:

```
'A' // simple character
'\u0041' // Unicode
'\x0041' // unsigned short hexadecimal
'\n' // escape sequence character
```

Table 2-1 summarizes the escape characters recognized by C#.

Table 2-1. Escape Sequence Characters

char	Meaning	Value
\'	Single quote	0x0027
\"	Double quote	0x0022
\\	Backslash	0x005C
\0	Null	0x0000
\a	Alert	0x0007
\b	Backspace	0x0008
\f	Form feed	0x000C
\n	New line	0x000A
\r	Carriage return	0x000D
\t	Horizontal tab	0x0009
\v	Vertical tab	0x000B

char conversions. An implicit conversion from a **char** to most numeric
types works; it's simply dependent on whether the numeric type can
accommodate an unsigned short. If it can't, an explicit conversion is
required.

bool type

C# Type	System Type	Size (bytes)
bool	System.Boolean	1/ 2

The **bool** type is a logical value, which can be assigned the literal **true** or
false.

Although Boolean values require only 1 bit (0 or 1), they occupy 1 byte of
storage since this is the minimum chunk addressing on most processor
architectures can work with. Each element in a array requires two bytes of
memory.

bool conversions. No conversions can be made from Booleans to numeric
types or vice versa.

object type

C# Type	System Type	Size (bytes)
object	System.Object	0/ 8 overhead

The `object` type is the ultimate base type for both value types and reference types. Value types have no storage overhead from `object`.
Reference types, which are stored on the heap, intrinsically require an
overhead. In the .NET runtime, a reference-type instance has an eight-byte
overhead, which stores the object's type and temporary information such
as its synchronization lock state or whether it has been fixed from movement by the garbage collector. Note that each reference to a reference
type instance uses four bytes of storage.

For more information on the `System.Object` type, see the section
"Common Types" in Chapter 3, *Programming the .NET Framework*.

string type

C# Type	System Type	Size (bytes)
string	System.String	20 minimum

The C# string represents an immutable sequence of Unicode characters and
aliases the `System.String` class (see the section "Strings" in Chapter 3).

Although `string` is a class, its use is so ubiquitous in programming that it
is given special privileges by both the C# compiler and .NET runtime.

Unlike other classes, a new instance can be created with a `string` literal:

```
string a = "Heat";
```

Strings can also be created with *verbatim* string literals. Verbatim string
literals start with a @, which indicates the string should be used verbatim,
even if it spans multiple lines or includes escape characters, i.e., "\". In
this example the pairs **a1** and **a2** represent the same string, and the pairs
b1 and **b2** represent the same string:

```
string a1 = "\\\\server\\fileshare\\helloworld.cs";
string a2 = @"\\server\fileshare\helloworld.cs";
Console.WriteLine(a1==a2); // Prints "True"

string b1 = "First Line\r\nSecond Line";
string b2 = @"First Line
Second Line";
Console.WriteLine(b1==b2); // Prints "True"
```

Types and Memory

The fundamental difference between value and reference types is how they are stored in memory.

Memory for value types

The memory of a value type instance simply holds a raw value, like a number or character. Value types are stored either on the stack or inline. A *stack* is a block of memory that grows each time a method is entered (because its local variables need storage space) and shrinks each time a method exits (because its local variables are no longer needed). *In-line* just means the value type is declared as part of a larger object, such as when it is a field in a class or member of an array.

Memory for reference types

The memory location of a reference type instance holds the address of an object on the heap. A reference type may be null, which means no object is referenced. During a program's execution, references are assigned to existing or new objects on the heap. An object on the heap remains in memory until the runtime's garbage collector determines it is no longer referenced, at which time the garbage collector discards the object and releases its memory.

Value types and reference types side by side

To create a value-type or reference-type instance, the constructor for the type may be called with the **new** keyword. A value-type constructor simply initializes an object. A reference-type constructor creates a new object on the heap and then initializes the object:

```
// Reference type declaration
class PointR {
  public int x, y;
}
// Value type declaration
struct PointV {
  public int x, y;
}
class Test {
  static void Main() {
    PointR a; // Local reference type variable, uses 4 bytes of
              // memory on the stack to hold address
    PointV b; // Local value type variable, uses 8 bytes of
              // memory on the stack for x and y
    a = new PointR(); // Assigns the reference to address of new
                      // instance of PointR allocated on the
```

```
                             // heap. The object on the heap uses 8
                             // bytes of memory for x and y, and an
                             // additional 8 bytes for core object
                             // requirements, such as storing the
                             // object's type  synchronization state
        b = new PointV();    // Calls the value type's default
                             // constructor.  The default constructor
                             // for both PointR and PointV will set
                             // each field to its default value, which
                             // will be 0 for both x and y.
        a.x = 7;
        b.x = 7;
      }
    }
    // At the end of the method the local variables a and b go out of
    // scope, but the new instance of a PointR remains in memory until
    // the garbage collector determines it is no longer referenced
```

Assignment to a reference type copies an object reference; assignment to a value type copies an object value:

```
        ...
        PointR c = a;
        PointV d = b;
        c.x = 9;
        d.x = 9;
        Console.WriteLine(a.x); // Prints 9
        Console.WriteLine(b.x); // Prints 7
      }
    }
```

As with this example, an object on the heap can be pointed at by many variables, whereas an object on the stack or inline can be accessed only via the variable it was declared with.

Unified Type System

C# provides a *unified type system*, whereby the **object** class is the ultimate base type for both reference and value types. This means that all types, apart from the occasionally used pointer types, share a basic set of characteristics.

Simple types are value types

In most languages, there is a strict distinction between simple types (**int**, **float**, etc.) and user-defined types (**Rectangle**, **Button**, etc.). In C#, simple types actually alias structs found in the **System** namespace. For instance, the **int** type aliases the **System.Int32** struct, and the **long** type aliases the **System.Int64** struct, etc. This means simple types have the same features you expect any user-defined type to have. For instance, you can call a method on an `int`:

```
int i = 3;
string s = i.ToString();
```

This is equivalent to:

```
// This is an explanatory version of System.Int32
namespace System {
  struct Int32 {
    ...
    public string ToString() {
      return ...;
    }
  }
}
// This is valid code, but we recommend you use the int alias
System.Int32 i = 5;
string s = i.ToString();
```

Value types expand the set of simple types

Creating an array of 1000 `int`s is highly efficient. This line allocates 1000 `int`s in one contiguous block of memory:

```
int[] iarr = new int [1000];
```

Similarly, creating an array of a value type `PointV` is also very efficient:

```
struct PointV {
  public int x, y
}
PointV[] pvarr = new PointV[1000];
```

Had you used a reference type `PointR`, you would have needed to instantiate 1000 individual points after instantiating the array:

```
class PointR {
  public int x, y;
}
PointR[] prarr = new PointR[1000];
for( int i=0; i<prarr.Length; i++ )
  prarr[i] = new PointR();
```

In Java, only the simple types (`int`, `float`, etc.) can be treated with this efficiency, while in C# you can expand the set of simple types by declaring a struct.

Furthermore, C#'s operators may be overloaded, so that operations typically applicable to simple types can also be applied to any class or struct, such as + and − (see the section "Expressions and Operators").

Boxing and unboxing value types

In C#, multiple reference types can share the characteristics of a common base type or interface, which allows reference types to be treated generically. This is very powerful. For instance, a method that takes a reference type R for a parameter works for any type that derives from R or implements R (see the section "Polymorphism").

To perform common operations on both reference and value types, each value type has a corresponding hidden reference type, which is automatically created when it is cast to a reference type. This process is called *boxing*.

In the following example, the `Queue` class can enqueue and dequeue any object (`object` is a reference type that is the base type of all types). You can put an `int` (a value type) in a queue, because an `int` can be boxed and unboxed to and from its corresponding reference type:

```
class Queue {
  ...
  void Enqueue(object o) {...}
  object Dequeue() {return ...}
}

Queue q = new Queue();
q.Enqueue(9); // box the int
int i = (int)q.Dequeue(); // unbox the int
```

When a value type is boxed, a new reference type is created to hold a copy of the value type. *Unboxing* copies the value from the reference type back into a value type. Unboxing requires an explicit cast, and a check is made to ensure the specified value type matches the type contained in the reference type, and an `InvalidCastException` is thrown if the check fails.

Function members of a value type don't actually override virtual function members of the class object or an implemented interface. However, a boxed value type overrides virtual function members.

Variables

A *variable* represents a typed storage location. A variable can be a local variable, a parameter, an array element (see the section "Arrays"), an instance field, or a static field (see the section "Instance and Static Members").

Every variable has an associated type, which essentially defines the possible values the variable can have and the operations that can be performed on that variable. C# is strongly typed, which means the set of operations that can be performed on a type is enforced at compile time, rather than runtime. In addition, C# is type-safe, which, with the help of runtime checking, ensures that a variable can be operated on only via the correct type (except in unsafe blocks; see the section "Unsafe Code").

Definite Assignment

Variables in C# (except in unsafe contexts) *must* be assigned a value before they are used. A variable is either explicitly assigned a value or automatically assigned a default value. Automatic assignment occurs for static fields, class instance fields, and array elements not explicitly assigned a value. For example:

```
using System;
class Test {
  int v;
  // Constructors that initalize an instance of a Test
  public Test() {} // v will be automatically assigned to 0
  public Test(int a) { // explicitly assign v a value
     v = a;
  }
  static void Main() {
    Test[] iarr = new Test [2]; // declare array
    Console.WriteLine(iarr[1]); // ok, elements assigned to null
    Test t;
    Console.WriteLine(t); // error, t not assigned
  }
}
```

The compiler generates a warning whenever a default value is assigned to a field that it can prove was never explicitly assigned. In the previous example, a warning is generated if the line `v = a` is commented out.

Default Values

The following table shows that, essentially, the default value for all primitive (or atomic) types is zero:

Type	Default Value
Numeric	`0`
Bool	`false`
Char	`'\0'`
Enum	`0`
Reference	`null`

The default value for each field in a complex (or composite) type is one of these aforementioned values.

Expressions and Operators

An expression is a sequence of operators and operands that specifies a computation. C# has unary operators, binary operators, and one ternary operator. Complex expressions can be built because an operand may itself be an expression, such as the operand (1 + 2) in the following example:

```
((1 + 2) / 3)
```

Operator Precedence

When an expression contains multiple operators, the *precedence* of the operators controls the order in which the individual operators are evaluated. When the operators are of the same precedence, their associativity determines their order of evaluation. Binary operators (except for assignment operators) are *left-associative* and are evaluated from left to right. The assignment operators, unary operators, and the conditional operator are *right-associative*, evaluated from right to left.

For example:

```
1 + 2 + 3 * 4
```

is evaluated as:

```
((1 + 2) +(3 * 4))
```

because * has a higher precedence than +, and + is a left-associative binary operator. You can insert brackets to change the default order of evaluation. C# also overloads operators, which means the same operator symbols can have different meanings in different contexts (e.g., primary, unary, etc.) or different meanings for different types.

Table 2-2 lists C#'s operators in order of precedence. Operators in the same box have the same precedence, and operators in *italic* may be overloaded for custom types (see the section "Operators").

Table 2-2. Operator Precedence Table

Category	Operators
Primary	Grouping: `(x)` Member access: `x.y` Struct pointer member access: `->` Method call: `f(x)` Indexing: `a[x]` *Post increment:* `x++` *Post decrement:* `x--` Constructor call: `new` Array stack allocation: `stackalloc` Type retrieval: `typeof` Struct size retrieval: `sizeof` Arithmetic check on: `checked` Arithmetic check off: `unchecked`
Unary	*Positive value of (passive):* + *Negative value of:* - *Not:* ! *Bitwise complement:* ~ *Pre increment:* ++x *Pre decrement:* --x Type cast: `(T)x` Value at address: * Address of value: &
Multiplicative	*Multiply:* * *Divide:* / *Division remainder:* %
Additive	*Add:* + *Subtract:* -
Shift	*Shift bits left:* << *Shift bits right:* >>
Relational	*Less than:* < *Greater than:* > *Less than or equal to:* <= *Greater than or equal to:* >= Type equality/compatibility: `is`
Equality	*Equals:* == *Not equals:* !=
Logical bitwise	*And:* & *Exclusive or:* ^ *Or:* |
Logical Boolean	And: && Or: || Ternary conditional: `?:` e.g. `int x = a > b ? 2 : 7;` s equivalent to: `int x; if (a > b) x = 2; else x = 7;`

Table 2-2. Operator Precedence Table (continued)

Category	Operators
Assignment	Assign/modify: = *= /= %= += -= <<= >>= &= ^= |=

Arithmetic Overflow Check Operators

Checked/unchecked operators:

```
checked (expression)
unchecked (expression)
```

Checked/unchecked statements:

```
checked statement-or-statement-block
unchecked statement-or-statement-block
```

The checked operator tells the runtime to generate an OverflowException if an integral expression exceeds the arithmetic limits of that type. The checked operator affects expressions with the ++, --, (unary)-, +, -, *, /, and explicit conversion operators () between integral types (see the section "Integral types"). Here's an example:

```
int a = 1000000;
int b = 1000000;

// Check an expression
int c = checked(a*b);

// Check every expression in a statement-block
checked {
    ...
    c = a * b;
    ...
}
```

The checked operator applies only to runtime expressions, because constant expressions are checked during compilation (though this can be turned off with the /checked [+/-] command-line compiler switch). The unchecked operator disables arithmetic checking at compile time and is seldom useful, but it can enable expressions such as this to compile:

```
const int signedBit = unchecked((int)0x80000000);
```

Statements

Execution off a C# program is specified by a series of *statements* that execute sequentially in the textual order in which they appear. All statements in a procedural-based language such as C# are executed for their effect. The two most basic kinds of statement in C# are the *declaration* and *expression* statements. C# also provides flow control statements for selection, looping and jumping. Finally C# provides statements for special purposes, such as locking memory or handling exceptions.

So that multiple statements can be grouped together, zero or more statements may be enclosed in braces ({ and }), to form a *statement block*. A statement block can be used anywhere a single statement is valid.

Expression Statements

[*variable* =]? *expression*;

An *expression statement* evaluates an expression either assigning its result to a variable or generating side-effects, (i.e., invocation, **new**, ++, or --). An expression statement ends in a semicolon (;). For example:

```
int x = 5 + 6; // assign result
x++; // side effect
int y = Math.Min(x, 20); // side effect and assign result
Math.Min (x, y); // discards result, but ok, there is a side effect
x == y; // error, has no side effect, and does not assign result
```

Declaration Statements

Variable declaration syntax:

type [*variable* [= *expression*]?]+ ;

Constant declaration syntax:

const *type* [*variable* = *constant-expression*]+ ;

A *declaration statement* declares a new variable. You can initialize a variable at the time of its declaration by optionally assigning it the result of an expression.

The scope of a local or constant variable extends to the end of the current block. You can't declare another local variable with the same name in the current or any nested blocks. For example:

```
bool a = true;
while(a) {
    int x = 5;
    if (x==5) {
        int y = 7;
        int x = 2; // error, x already defined
    }
    Console.WriteLine(y); // error, y is out of scope
}
```

A *constant declaration* is like a variable declaration, except that the value of the variable can't be changed after it has been declared:

```
const double speedOfLight = 2.99792458E08;
speedOfLight+=10; // error
```

Empty Statements

```
;
```

The *empty statement* does nothing. It is used as placeholder when no operations need to be performed, but a statement is nevertheless required. For example:

```
while(!thread.IsAlive);
```

Selection Statements

C# has many ways to conditionally control the flow of program execution. This section covers the simplest two constructs, the `if-else` statement and the `switch` statement. In addition, C# also provides a conditional operator and loop statements that conditionally execute based on a Boolean expression. Finally, C# provides object-oriented ways of conditionally controlling the flow of execution, namely virtual method invocations and delegate invocations.

if-else statement

```
if (Boolean-expression)
  statement-or-statement-block
[ else
  statement-or-statement-block ]?
```

An `if-else` statement executes code depending on whether a Boolean expression is `true`. Unlike C, C# only permits a Boolean expression. For example:

```
int Compare(int a, int b) {
    if (a>b)
       return 1;
    else if (a<b)
       return -1;
    return 0;
}
```

switch statement

```
switch (expression) {
[ case constant-expression : statement* ] *
[ default : statement*] ?
}
```

switch statements let you branch program execution based on the value of a variable. switch statements can result in cleaner code than if you use multiple if statements, because the controlling is evaluated only once. For instance:

```
void Award(int x)
   switch(x)
     case 1:
       Console.WriteLine("Winner!");
       break;
     case 2:
       Console.WriteLine("Runner-up");
       break;
     case 3:
     case 4:
       Console.WriteLine("Highly commended");
       break;
     default:
       Console.WriteLine("Don't quit your day job!");
       break;
   }
 }
```

The switch statement can evaluate only a predefined type (including the string type) or enum, though user-defined types may provide an implicit conversion to these types.

After a particular case statement is executed, control doesn't automatically continue to the next statement or break out of the switch statement. Instead, you must explicitly control execution, typically by ending each case statement with a jump statement. The options are:

- Use the break statement to jump to the end of the switch statement (this is by far the most common option).

- Use the goto case <constant expression> or goto default statements to jump to either another case statement or the default case statement.

- Use any other jump statement, namely return, throw, continue, or goto label.

Unlike in Java and C++, the end of a case statement must explicitly state where to go next. There is no error-prone "default fall through" behavior, so not specifying a **break** results in the next **case** statement being executed:

```
void Greet(string title) {
  switch (title) {
    case null:
      Console.WriteLine("And you are?");
      goto default;
    case "King":
      Console.WriteLine("Greetings your highness");
      // error, should specify break, otherwise...
    default :
      Console.WriteLine("How's it hanging?");
      break;
  }
}
```

Loop Statements

C# enables a group of statements to be executed repeatedly using the **while**, **do while** and **for** statements.

while loops

> while (*Boolean-expression*)
>   *statement* or *statement-block*

while loops repeatedly execute a statement block while a given Boolean expression remains **true**. The expression is tested before the statement block is executed:

```
int i = 0;
while (i<5) {
  i++;
}
```

do-while loops

> do
>   *statement o -statement-block*
> while (*Boolean-expression*);

do-while loops differ functionally from **while** loops only in that they test the controlling Boolean expression after the statement block has executed. Here's an example:

```
int i = 0;
do
  i++;
while (i<5);
```

for loops

```
for (statement?; Boolean-expression?; statement?)
  statement-or-statement-block
```

`for` loops can be more convenient than `while` loops when you need to maintain an iterator value. As in Java and C, `for` loops contain three parts. The first part is a statement executed before the loop begins, and by convention, it initializes an iterator variable. The second part is a Boolean expression that, while `true`, permits the statement block to execute. The third part is a statement that is executed after each iteration of the statement block, and by convention, iterates an iterator variable. Here's an example:

```
for (int i=0; i<10; i++)
  Console.WriteLine(i);
```

Any of the three parts of the `for` statement may be omitted. You can implement an infinite loop like this, though alternatively a `while (true)` statement has the same result:

```
for (;;)
  Console.WriteLine("Hell ain't so bad");
```

foreach loops

```
foreach ( type-value in IEnumerable )
  statement or statement-block
```

It's common to use for loops to iterate over a collection, so C#, like Visual Basic, includes a `foreach` statement. For instance, instead of doing this:

```
for (int i=0; i<dynamite.Length; i++)
  Console.WriteLine(dynamite [i]);
```

you can do this:

```
foreach (Stick stick in dynamite)
  Console.WriteLine(stick);
```

The `foreach` statement works on any collection (including arrays). Although not strictly necessary, all collections leverage this functionality by supporting the `IEnumerable` and `IEnumerable` interfaces, which are explained in the section "Collections" in Chapter 3. Here is an equivalent way to iterate over the collection:

```
IEnumerator ie = dynamite.GetEnumerator();
while (ie.MoveNext()) {
  Stick stick = (Stick)ie.Current;
  Console.WriteLine(stick);
}
```

jump Statements

The C# jump statements are: break, continue, goto, return, and throw. All jump statements obey sensible restrictions imposed by try statements (see the section "try Statements and Exceptions"). First, a jump out of a try block always executes the try's finally block before reaching the target of the jump. Second, a jump can't be made from the inside to the outside of a finally block.

break statement

```
break;
```

The break statement transfers execution to the enclosing while loop, for loop, or switch statement block, to the next statement block.

```
int x = 0;
while (true) {
  x++;
  if (x>5)
    break; // break from the loop
}
```

continue statement

```
continue;
```

The continue statement forgoes the remaining statements in the loop and makes an early start on the next iteration:

```
int x = 0;
int y = 0;
while (y<100) {
  x++;
  if ((x%7)==0)
    continue; // continue with next iteration
  y++;
}
```

goto statement

```
goto statement-label;
goto case-constant;
```

The goto statement transfers execution to another *label* within the statement block. A label statement is just a placeholder in a method:

```
int x = 4;
start:
x++;
if (x==5)
 goto start;
```

The goto case statement transfers execution to another case *label* in a switch block (as explained in the "switch statement" section).

return statement

```
return expression?;
```

The return statement exits a method and if the method is non-void, it must return an expression of the method's return type:

```
int CalcX(int a) {
   int x = a * 100;
   return x; // return to the calling method with value
}
```

throw statement

```
throw exception-expression?;
```

The throw statement throws an Exception to indicate that an abnormal condition has occurred (see the section "try Statements and Exceptions").

```
if (w==null)
   throw new Exception("w can't be null");
```

lock statement

```
lock (expression)
statement-or-statement-block
```

The lock statement is actually a syntactic shortcut for calling the Enter and Exit methods of the Monitor class (see the section "Threading" in Chapter 3).

Organizing Types

A C# program is basically a group of types. These types are defined in *files*, organized by *namespaces*, compiled into *modules*, and then grouped into an *assembly*.

Generally, these organizational units overlap: an assembly can contain many namespaces, and a namespace can be spread across several assemblies. A module can be part of many assemblies, and an assembly can contain many modules. A source file can contain many namespaces, and a namespace can span many source files. For more information, see the section "Assemblies" in Chapter 3.

Files

File organization is of almost no significance to the C# compiler: an entire project can be merged into a single *.cs* file and still compile successfully (preprocessor statements are the only exception to this). However, it's generally tidy to have one type in one file, with a filename that matches the name of the class and a directory name that matches the name of the class's namespace.

Namespaces

Namespace declaration syntax:

```
namespace name+ * {
 using-statement*
 [namespace-declaration | type-declaration] * †
}
```

A *namespace* enables you to group related types into a hierarchical categorization. Generally the first name in a namespace name is the name of your organization, followed by names that group types with finer granularity. For example:

```
namespace MyCompany.MyProduct.Drawing {
  class Point {int x, y, z}
  delegate void PointInvoker(Point p);
}
```

Nesting namespaces

You may also nest namespace declarations instead of using dots. This example is semantically identical to the previous example:

```
namespace MyCompany {
  namespace MyProduct {
    namespace Drawing {
      class Point {int x, y, z}
      delegate void PointInvoker(Point p);
    }
  }
}
```

---

* Dot-delimited.

† No delimiters.

Using a type with its fully qualified name

The complete name of a type includes its namespace name. To use the `Point` class from another namespace, you may refer to it with its fully qualified name:

```
namespace TestProject {
  class Test {
    static void Main() {
      MyCompany.MyProduct.Drawing.Point x;
    }
  }
}
```

using keyword

The `using` keyword is a convenient way to avoid using the fully qualified names of types in other namespaces. This example is semantically identical to the previous example:

```
namespace TestProject {
  using MyCompany.MyProduct.Drawing;
  class Test {
    static void Main() {
      Point x;
    }
  }
}
```

Aliasing types and namespaces

Type names must be unique within a namespace. To avoid naming conflicts without having to use fully qualified names, C# allows you to specify an alias for a type or namespace. Here is an example:

```
using sys = System;        // Namespace alias
using txt = System.String; // Type alias
class Test {
  static void Main() {
    txt s = "Hello, World!";
    sys.Console.WriteLine(s); // Hello, World!
    sys.Console.WriteLine(s.GetType()); // System.String
  }
}
```

Global namespace

The outermost level within which all namespaces and types are implicitly declared is called the *global namespace*. When a type isn't explicitly declared within a namespace, it can be used without qualification from any other namespace, since it is a member of the global namespace.

However, it is always good practice to organize types within logical namespaces

Inheritance

A C# class can *inherit* from another class to extend or customize that class. A class can only inherit from a single class but can be inherited by many classes, thus forming a class hierarchy. At the root of any class hierarchy is the `object` class, which all objects implicitly inherit from. Inheriting from a class requires specifying the class to inherit from in the class declaration, using the C++ colon notation:

```
class Location { // Implicitly inherits from object
  string name;

  // The constructor that initializes Location
  public Location(string name) {
    this.name = name;
  }
  public string Name {get {return name;}}
  public void Display() {
    Console.WriteLine(Name);
  }
}
class URL : Location { // Inherit from Location
  public void Navigate() {
    Console.WriteLine("Navigating to "+Name);
  }
  // The constructor for URL, which calls Location's constructor
  public URL(string name) : base(name) {}
}
```

URL has all the members of **Location**, and a new member, **Navigate**:

```
class Test {
  static void Main() {
    URL u = new URL("http://microsoft.com");
    u.Display();
    u.Navigate();
  }
}
```

The specialized class and general class are referred to as either the *derived class* and *base class* or the *subclass* and *superclass.*

Class Conversions

A class D may be implicitly *upcast* to the class B it derives from, and a class B may be explicitly *downcast* to a class D that derives from it. For instance:

```
URL u = new URL();
Location l = u; // upcast
u = (URL)l; // downcast
```

If the downcast fails, an `InvalidCastException` is thrown.

as operator

The `as` operator allows a downcast to be made that evaluates to `null` if the downcast fails:

```
u = l as URL;
```

is operator

The `is` operator can test if an object is or derives from a specified class (or implements an interface). It is often used to perform a test before a downcast:

```
if (l is URL)
  ((URL)l).Navigate();
```

Polymorphism

Polymorphism is the ability to perform the same operation on many types, as long as each type shares a common subset of characteristics. C# custom types exhibit polymorphism by inheriting classes and implementing interfaces (see the section "Interfaces").

In the following example, the `Show` method can perform the operation `Display` on both a `URL` and a `LocalFile`, because both types inherit the characteristics of `Location`:

```
class LocalFile : Location {
  public void Execute() {
    Console.WriteLine("Executing "+Name);
  }
  // The constructor for LocalFile, which calls URL's constructor
  public LocalFile(string name) : base(name) {}
}
class Test {
  static void Main() {
    URL u = new URL();
    LocalFile l = new LocalFile();
    Show(u);
```

```
      Show(1);
    }
    public static void Show(Location loc) {
      Console.Write("Location is: ");
      loc.Display();
    }
  }
```

Virtual Function Members

A key aspect of polymorphism is that each type can implement a shared characteristic in its own way. One way to permit such flexibility is for a base class to declare function members as virtual. Derived classes can provide their own implementations for any function members marked virtual in the base class (see the section "Interfaces"):

```
class Location {
  public virtual void Display() {
    Console.WriteLine(Name);
    }
    . . .
}
class URL : Location {
  // chop off the http:// at the start
  public override void Display() {
    Console.WriteLine(Name.Substring(6));
  }
  . . .
}
```

URL now has a custom way of displaying itself. The Show method of the Test class in the previous section will now call the new implementation of Display. The signatures of the overridden method and the virtual method must be identical, but unlike Java and C++, the override keyword is also required.

Abstract Classes and Members

A class can be declared *abstract*. An abstract class may have abstract members, which are function members without implementation that are implicitly virtual. In earlier examples, we specified a Navigate method for the URL type and an Execute method for the LocalFile type. You can, instead, declare Location an abstract class with an abstract method called Launch:

```
abstract class Location {
  public abstract void Launch();
}
class URL : Location {
  public override void Launch() {
```

```
      Console.WriteLine("Run Internet Explorer...");
    }
  }
  class LocalFile : Location {
    public override void Launch() {
      Console.WriteLine("Run Win32 Program...");
    }
  }
```

A derived class must override all its inherited **abstract** members or must itself be declared **abstract**. An **abstract** class can't be instantiated. For instance, if **LocalFile** doesn't override **Launch**, **LocalFile** itself must be declared **abstract**, perhaps to allow **Shortcut** and **PhysicalFile** to derive from it.

Sealed Classes

A class can prevent other classes from inheriting from it by specifying the **sealed** modifier in the class declaration:

```
sealed class Math {
  ...
}
```

The most common scenario for sealing a class is when that class comprises only static members, such as is the case with the **Math** class of the base class library. Another effect of sealing a class is that it enables the compiler to turn all virtual method invocations made on that class into faster nonvirtual method invocations.

Hiding Inherited Members

Aside from its use for calling a constructor, the **new** keyword can also hide the data members, function members, and type members of a base class. Overriding a virtual method with the **new** keyword hides, rather than overrides, the base class implementation of the method:

```
class B {
  public virtual void Foo() {}
}
class D : B {
  public override void Foo() {}
}
class N : D {
  public new void Foo() {} // hides D's Foo
}
N n = new N();
n.Foo(); // calls N's Foo
((D)n).Foo(); // calls D's Foo
((B)n).Foo(); // calls D's Foo
```

A method declaration with the same signature as its base class must explicitly state whether it overrides or hides the inherited member.

Versioning Virtual Function Members

In C#, a method is compiled with a flag that is true if the method overrides the virtual method of a class or interface. This flag is important for versioning. Suppose that you write a class that derives from a base class in the .NET Framework and then deploy your application to a client computer. The client later upgrades the .NET Framework, and the .NET base class now contains a virtual method that happens to match the signature of one of your methods in the derived class:

```
class B { // written by the library people
  virtual void Foo() {...} // added in latest update
}
class D : B { // written by you
  void Foo() {...}
}
```

In most object-oriented languages, such as Java, methods are not compiled with this flag, so a derived class's method with the same signature is *assumed* to override the base class's virtual method. This means a virtual call is made to type D's Foo method, even though D's Foo is unlikely to have been implemented according to the specification intended by the author of type B. This can easily break your application. In C#, the flag for D's Foo will be false, so the runtime knows to treat D's Foo as new, which ensures that your application will function as it was originally intended. When you get the chance to recompile with the latest framework, you can add the new modifier to Foo, or perhaps rename Foo to something else.

Access Modifiers

To promote encapsulation, a type or type member may hide itself from other types or other assemblies, by adding one of the following five access modifiers to the declaration:

public
> The type or type member is fully accessible. This is the implicit accessibility for enum members (see the section "Enums") and interface members (see the section "Interfaces").

internal

The type or type member in assembly A is accessible only from within A. This is the default accessibility for nonnested types, so may be omitted.

private

The type member in type T is accessible only from within T. This is the default accessibility for class and struct members, so it may be omitted.

protected

The type member in class C is accessible only from within C or from within a class that derives from C.

protected internal

The type member in class C and assembly A is accessible only from within C, from within a class that derives from C, or from within A. Note that C# has no concept of **protected** and **internal**, where a type member in class C and assembly A is accessible only from within C or from within a class that derives from C and is within A.

Note that a type member may be a nested type. Here is an example that uses access modifiers:

```
// Assembly1.dll
using System;
public class A {
  private int x=5;
  public void Foo() {Console.WriteLine (x);}
  protected static void Goo() {}
  protected internal class NestedType {}
}
internal class B {
  private void Hoo () {
    A a1 = new A (); // ok
    Console.WriteLine(a1.x); // error, A.x is private
    A.NestedType n; // ok, A.NestedType is internal
    A.Goo(); // error, A's Goo is protected
  }
}

// Assembly2.exe (references Assembly1.dll)
using System;
class C : A { // C defaults to internal
  static void Main() { // Main defaults to private
    A a1 = new A(); // ok
    a1.Foo(); // ok
    C.Goo(); // ok, inherits A's protected static member
    new A.NestedType(); // ok, A.NestedType is protected
    new B(); // error, Assembly 1's B is internal
```

```
      Console.WriteLine(x); // error, A's x is private
   }
}
```

Restrictions on Access Modifiers

A type or type member can't declare itself to be more accessible than any of the types it uses in its declaration. For instance, a class can't be `public` if it derives from an internal class, or a method can't be protected if the type of one of its parameters is internal to the assembly. The rationale behind this restriction is that whatever is accessible to another type is actually usable by that type.

In addition, access modifiers can't be used when they conflict with the purpose of inheritance modifiers. For example, a `virtual` (or `abstract`) member can't be declared `private`, since it would then be impossible to override. Similarly, a sealed class can't define new protected members, since there is no class that can benefit from this accessibility.

Finally, to maintain the contract of a base class, a function member with the `override` modifier must have the same accessibility as the `virtual` member it overrides.

Classes and Structs

Class declaration syntax:

```
attributes? access-modifier?
new? [ abstract | sealed ]?
class class-name [
: base-class | : interface+ | : base-class, interface+ ]?
{ class-members }
```

Struct declaration syntax:

```
attributes? access-modifier?
new?
struct struct-name [: interface+]?
{ struct-members }
```

A class or struct combines data, functions, and nested types into a new type, which is a key building block of C# applications. The body of a class or struct is comprised of three kinds of members: data, function, and type.

Data members

Includes fields, constants, events. The most common data members are fields. Events are a special case, since they combine data and functionality in the class or struct (see the section "Events").

Function members

Includes methods, properties, indexers, operators, constructors, and destructors. Note that all function members are either specialized types of methods or are implemented with one or more specialized types of methods.

Type members

Includes nested types. Types can be nested to control their accessibility (see the section "Access Modifiers").

Here's an example:

```
class ExampleClass {
    int x; // data member
    void Foo() {} // function member
    struct MyNestedType  {} // type member
}
```

Differences Between Classes and Structs

Classes differ from structs in the following ways:

- A class is a reference type; a struct is a value type. Consequently, structs typically simple types, whereas value-type semantics are desirable (e.g., assignment copies a value rather than a reference).

- A class fully supports inheritance (see the earlier section, "Inheritance"). A struct inherits from **object** and is implicitly sealed. Both classes and structs can implement interfaces.

- A class can have a destructor; a struct can't.

- A class can define a custom parameterless constructor and initialize instance fields; a struct can't. The default parameterless constructor for a struct initializes each field with a default value (effectively zero). If a struct declares a constructor(s), all its fields must be assigned in that constructor call.

Instance and Static Members

Data members and function members may be either instance (default) or static members. Instance members are associated with an instance of a type, whereas static members are associated with the type itself. Furthermore, invocation of static members from outside their enclosing type

requires specifying the type name. In this example, the instance method
`PrintName` prints the name of a particular `Panda`, while the static method
`PrintSpeciesName` prints the name shared by all `Pandas` in the application (`AppDomain`):

```
class Panda {
  string name;
  static string speciesName = "Ailuropoda melanoleuca";
  // Initializes Panda(see Instance Constructors)
  public Panda(string name) {
    this.name = name;
  }
  public void PrintName() {
    Console.WriteLine(name);
  }
  public static void PrintSpeciesName() {
    Console.WriteLine(speciesName);
  }
}
class Test {
  static void Main() {
    Panda.PrintSpeciesName(); // invoke static method
    Panda p = new Panda("Petey");
    p.PrintName(); // invoke instance method
  }
}
```

Fields

> *attributes*? *access-modifier*?
>
> new?
>
> static?
>
> readonly?
>
> *type* [*field-name* [= *expression*]?]+ ;

Fields hold data for a class or struct. Fields are also referred to as member
variables:

```
class MyClass {
  int x;
  float y = 1, z = 2;
  static readonly int MaxSize = 10;
  ...
}
```

As the name suggests, the **readonly** modifier ensures a field can't be
modified after it's assigned. Such a field is termed a *read-only field*. A
read-only field is always evaluated at runtime, not at compile time. To
compile, a nonread-only field must be assigned in its declaration or within
the type's constructor (see the section "Instance Constructors"). Nonread-
only fields merely generate a warning when left unassigned.

Constants

```
attributes? access-modifier?
new?
const type [ constant-name = constant-expression ]+;
```

The *type* must be a predefined type of: sbyte, byte, short, ushort, int, uint, long, ulong, float, double, decimal, bool, char, string, or enum.

A *constant* is a field that is evaluated at compile time and is implicitly static. The logical consequence of this is that a constant can't defer evaluation to a method or constructor and can only be one of a few built-in types (see the preceding syntax definition).

```
public const double PI = 3.14159265358979323846;
```

The benefit of a constant is that since it is evaluated at compile time, the compiler can perform additional optimization. For instance:

```
public static double Circumference(double radius) {
  return 2 * Math.PI * radius;
}
```

Evaluates to:

```
public static double Circumference(double radius) {
  return 6.2831853071795862 * radius;
}
```

Versioning with constants

A readonly field isn't optimized by the compiler but is more versionable. For instance, suppose there is a mistake with PI, and Microsoft releases a patch to their library that contains the Math class, which is deployed to each client computer. If software using the Circumference method is already deployed on a client machine, the mistake isn't fixed until you recompile your application with the latest version of the Math class. With a readonly field, however, this mistake is automatically fixed the next time the client application is executed. Generally this scenario occurs when a field value changes not as a result of a mistake, but simply because of an upgrade, such as a change in the value of the MaxThreads constant from 500 to 1000.

Properties

```
attributes? access-modifier?
[override | new? [virtual | abstract | static]? ]?
unsafe?
type property-name{ [
 attributes? get statement-block | // read-only
 attributes? set statement-block | // write-only
 attributes? get statement-block // read-write
 attributes? set statement-block |
] }
```

abstract accessors don't specify an implementation, so they replace a statement block with a semicolon. Also see the section "Restrictions on Access Modifiers."

A *property* can be characterized as an object-oriented field. Properties promote encapsulation by allowing a class or struct to control access to its data and by hiding the internal representation of the data. For instance:

```
public class Well {
   decimal dollars; // private field
   public int Cents {
     get { return(int)(dollars * 100); }
     set {
       // value is an implicit variable in a set
       if (value>=0) // typical validation code
          dollars = (decimal)value/100;
     }
   }
}
class Test {
   static void Main() {
     Well w = new Well();
     w.Cents = 25; // set
     int x = w.Cents; // get
     w.Cents += 10; // get and set(throw a dime in the well)
   }
}
```

The get accessor returns a value of the property's type. The set accessor has an implicit parameter value that is of the property's type.

Many languages loosely implement properties with a `get` or `set` method convention, and in fact C# properties are compiled to `get_XXX` or `set_XXX` methods, which is their representation in MSIL; for example:

```
public int get_Cents {...}
public void set_Cents (int value) {...}
```

Simple property accessors are inlined by the JIT (just-in-time compiler), which means there is no performance difference between a property access and a field access. Inlining is an optimization that replaces a method call with the body of that method.

Indexers

> *attributes? access-modifier?*
> [override | new? [virtual | abstract]?]?
> unsafe?
> *type* this [*attributes? [type arg]+*] {
> *attributes?* get *statement-block* | *// read-only*
> *attributes?* set *statement-block* | *// write-only*
> *attributes?* get *statement-block // read-write*
> *attributes?* set *statement-block* |
> }

`abstract` accessors don't specify an implementation, so they replace a statement block with a semicolon. Also see the section "Restrictions on Access Modifiers."

An *indexer* provides a natural way to index elements in a class or struct that encapsulates a collection, using the open and closed bracket [] syntax of the array type. For example:

```
public class ScoreList {
  int[] scores = new int [5];
  // indexer
  public int this[int index] {
    get {
      return scores[index]; }
    set {
      if(value >= 0 && value <= 10)
        scores[index] = value;
    }
  }
  // property (read-only)
  public int Average {
    get {
      int sum = 0;
      foreach(int score in scores)
```

```
            sum += score;
        return sum / scores.Length;
      }
    }
  }
  class IndexerTest {
    static void Main() {
      ScoreList sl = new ScoreList();
      sl[0] = 9;
      sl[1] = 8;
      sl[2] = 7;
      sl[3] = sl[4] = sl[1];
      System.Console.WriteLine(sl.Average);
    }
  }
```

A type may declare multiple indexers that take different parameters.

Indexers are compiled to `get_Item (...)`/`set_Item (...)` methods, which is their representation in MSIL:

```
public Story get_Item (int index) {...}
public void set_Item (int index, Story value) {...}
```

Methods

Method declaration syntax:

```
attributes? access-modifier?
[ override | new? [ virtual | abstract | static extern? ]? ]?
unsafe?
[ void | type ] method-name (parameter-list)
statement-block
```

Parameter list syntax:

```
[ attributes? [ref | out]? type arg ]*
[ params attributes? type[] arg ]?
```

`abstract` and `extern` methods don't contain a method body. Also see the earlier section "Restrictions on Access Modifiers."

All C# code executes in a *method* or a special form of a method (constructors, destructors, and operators are special types of methods, and properties and indexers are internally implemented with `get`/`set` methods).

Signatures

A method's *signature* is characterized by the type and modifier of each parameter in its parameter list. The parameter modifiers `ref` and `out` allow arguments to be passed by reference rather than be passed by value.

Passing arguments by value

By default, arguments in C# are passed by value, which is by far the most common case. This means a copy of the value is created when passed to the method:

```
static void Foo(int p) {++p;}
static void Main() {
  int x = 8;
  Foo(x); // make a copy of the value type x
  Console.WriteLine(x); // x will still be 8
}
```

Assigning `p` a new value doesn't change the contents of `x`, since `p` and `x` reside in *different* memory locations.

ref modifier

To pass by reference, C# provides the parameter modifier `ref`. Using this modifier allows `p` and `x` to refer to the same memory locations:

```
static void Foo(ref int p) {++p;}
static void Test() {
  int x = 8;
  Foo(ref x); // send reference of x to Foo
  Console.WriteLine(x); // x is now 9
}
```

Now, assigning `p` a new value changes the contents of `x`. This is usually why you want to pass by reference, though occasionally it is an efficient technique with which to pass large structs. Notice how the `ref` modifier is required in the method call, as well as in the method declaration. This makes it very clear what's going on and also removes ambiguity since parameter modifiers change the signature of a method (see the section "Signatures").

out modifier

C# is a language that enforces the requirement that variables be assigned before use, so it also provides the `out` modifier, which is the natural complement of the `ref` modifier. While a `ref` modifier requires that a variable be assigned a value before being passed to a method, the `out` modifier requires that a variable be assigned a value before returning from a method:

```
using System;
class Test {
  static void Split(string name, out string firstNames,
                    out string lastName) {
    int i = name.LastIndexOf(' ');
    firstNames = name.Substring(0, i);
    lastName = name.Substring(i+1);
  }
  static void Main() {
    string a, b;
    Split("Nuno Bettencourt", out a, out b);
    Console.WriteLine("FirstName:{0}, LastName:{1}", a, b);
  }
}
```

params modifier

The **params** parameter modifier may be specified on the last parameter of a method so that the method can accept any number of parameters of a particular type. For example:

```
using System;
class Test {
  static int Add(params int[] iarr) {
    int sum = 0;
    foreach(int i in iarr)
      sum += i;
    return sum;
  }
  static void Main() {
    int i = Add(1, 2, 3, 4);
    Console.WriteLine(i); // 10
  }
}
```

Overloading methods

A type may overload methods (have multiple methods with the same name) so long as the signatures are different. For example, the following methods can coexist in the same type:

```
void Foo(int x);
viod Foo(double x);
void Foo(int x, float y);
void Foo(float x, int y);
void Foo(ref int x);
void Foo(out int x);
```

However, the following pairs of methods can't coexist in the same type, since the **return** type and **params** modifier don't qualify as part of a method's signature.

```
void Foo(int x);
float Foo(int x); // compile error
void Goo (int[] x);
void Goo (params int[] x); // compile error
```

Operators

Overloadable operators:

+ - ! ~ ++ -- + -

*(binary only) / % & (binary only)

| ^ << >> ++ != > <

>= <=

Literals doubling as overloadable operators:

true false

C# lets you overload operators to work with operands that are custom classes or structs using operators. An *operator* is a static method with the keyword operator preceding the operator to be overloaded (instead of a method name), parameters representing the operands, and return type representing the result of an expression.

Implementing value equality

The most common operators to overload are the == and != operators, which are used to implement value equality, as opposed to referential equality. If two objects have the same value, they are considered equivalent, even if they refer to objects in different memory locations.

In the following scenario you should override the virtual **Equals** method to route its functionality to the == operator. This allows a class to be later treated as one of its base classes (see the section "Polymorphism"), yet still be tested for value equality. It also provides compatibility with other .NET languages that don't overload operators.

```
class Note
  int value;
  public Note(int semitonesFromA) {
    value = semitonesFromA;
  }
  public static bool operator ==(Note x, Note y) {
    return x.value == y.value;
  }
  public static bool operator !=(Note x, Note y) {
    return x.value != y.value;
  }
  public override bool Equals(object o) {
```

```
      if(!(o is Note))
        return false;
      return this ==(Note)o;
    }
  }
Note a = new Note(4);
Note b = new Note(4);
Object c = a;
Object d = b;

// To compare a and b by reference
Console.WriteLine((object)a ==(object)b; // false

//To compare a and b by value:
Console.WriteLine(a == b); // true

//To compare c and d by reference:
Console.WriteLine(c == d); // false

//To compare c and d by value:
Console.WriteLine(c.Equals(d)); // true
```

Logically paired operators

The C# compiler enforces the rule that operators that are logical pairs must both be defined. These operators are == and !=; < and >; and <= and >=.

Custom implicit and explicit conversions

As explained in the earlier section "Types," the rationale behind *implicit* conversions is they are guaranteed to succeed and not lose information during the conversion. Conversely, an *explicit* conversion is required either when runtime circumstances determine if the conversion succeeds or if information is lost during the conversion. In the following example, we define conversions between the musical Note type and a double (which represents the frequency in hertz of that note):

```
...
// Convert to hertz
public static implicit operator double(Note x) {
   return 440*Math.Pow(2,(double)x.value/12);
}

// Convert from hertz(only accurate to nearest semitone)
public static explicit operator Note(double x) {
   return new Note((int)(0.5+12*(Math.Log(x/440)/Math.Log(2))));
}
...

Note n =(Note)554.37; // explicit conversion
double x = n; // implicit conversion
```

Three-state logic operators

The `true` and `false` keywords are used as operators when defining types with *three-state logic,* to enable these types to seamlessly work with constructs that take Boolean expressions, namely the `if`, `do`, `while`, `for`, and conditional (`?:`) statements. The `System.Data.SQLTypes.SQLBoolean` struct provides this functionality:

```
public struct SQLBoolean ... {
  ...
  public static bool operator true(SQLBoolean x) {
    return x.value == 1;
  }
  public static bool operator false(SQLBoolean x) {
    return x.value == -1;
  }
  public static SQLBoolean operator !(SQLBoolean x) {
    return new SQLBoolean(- x.value);
  }
  public bool IsNull {
    get { return value == 0;}
  }
  ...
}
class Test {
  void Foo(SQLBoolean a) {
    if (a)
      Console.WriteLine("True");
    else if (! a)
      Console.WriteLine("False");
    else
      Console.WriteLine("Null");
  }
}
```

Indirectly overloadable operators

The `&&` and `||` operators are automatically evaluated from `&` and `|` so they don't need to be overloaded. The `[]` operators can be customized with indexers (see the section "Indexers"). The assignment operator `=` can't be overloaded, but all other assignment operators are automatically evaluated from their corresponding binary operators (e.g., `+=` is evaluated from `+`).

Instance Constructors

```
attributes? access-modifier?
unsafe?
class-name (parameter-list)
[ :[ base | this ] (argument-list) ]?
statement-block
```

An instance of a *constructor* allows you to specify the code to be executed when a class or struct is instantiated. A class constructor first creates a new instance of that class on the heap and then performs initialization, while a struct constructor merely performs initialization.

Unlike ordinary methods, a constructor has the same name as the class or struct in which it is declared and has no return type:

```
class MyClass {
  public MyClass() {
    // initialization code
  }
}
```

A class or struct can overload constructors and may call one of its overloaded constructors before executing its method body using the **this** keyword:

```
class MyClass {
  public int x;
  public MyClass() : this(5) {}
  public MyClass(int v) {
    x = v;
  }
}
MyClass m1 = new MyClass();
MyClass m2 = new MyClass(10);
Console.WriteLine(m1.x) // 5
Console.Writeline(m2.x) // 10;
```

If a class does not define any constructors, an implicit parameterless constructor is created. A struct can't define a parameterless constructor, since a constructor that initializes each field with a default value (effectively zero) is always implicitly defined.

Calling base class constructors

A class constructor must call one of its base class constructors first. In the case where the base class has a parameterless constructor, that constructor is called implicitly. In the case where the base class provides only constructors that require parameters, the derived class constructor must explicitly call one of the base class constructors, using the base keyword. A constructor may also call an overloaded constructor (which calls base for it):

```
class B {
  public int x ;
  public B(int a) {
    x = a;
  }
  public B(int a, int b) {
```

```
    x = a * b;
  }
  // Notice how all of B's constructors need parameters
}
class D : B {
  public D() : this(7) {} // call an overloaded constructor
  public D(int a) : base(a) {} // call a base class constructor
}
```

Field initialization order

Another useful way to perform initialization is to assign fields an initial value in their declaration:

```
class MyClass {
  int x = 5;
}
```

Field assignments are performed before the constructor is executed and are initialized in the textual order in which they appear. For classes, every field assignment in each class in the inheritance chain is executed before any of the constructors is executed, from the least derived to the most derived class.

Constructor access modifiers

A class or struct may choose any access modifier for a constructor. It is occasionally useful to specify a private constructor to prevent a class from being constructed. This is appropriate for utility classes made up entirely of static members, such as the System.Math class.

Static Constructors

```
attributes?
static class-name ( )
statement-block
```

A *static constructor* allows initialization code to be executed before the first instance of a class or struct is created, or before any static member of the class or struct is accessed. A class or struct can only define one static constructor, and it must be parameterless and have the same name as the class or struct:

```
class Test {
   static Test() {
       Console.WriteLine("Test Initialized");
   }
}
```

Base class constructor order

Consistent with instance constructors, static constructors respect the inheritance chain, so each static constructor from the least derived to the most derived is called.

Static field initialization order

Consistent with instance fields, each static field assignment is made before any of the static constructors is called, and the fields are initialized in the textual order in which they appear:

```
class Test {
  public static int x = 5;
  public static void Foo() {}
  static Test() {
    Console.WriteLine("Test Initialized");
  }
}
```

Accessing either `Test.x` or `Test.Foo` assigns 5 to `x`, and prints `Test Initialized`.

Nondeterminism of static constructor calls

Static constructors can't be called explicitly, and the runtime may invoke them well before they are first used. Programs shouldn't make any assumptions about the timing of a static constructor's invocation. In the following example, `Test Initialized` can be printed after `Test2 Initialized`:

```
class Test2 {
  public static void Foo() {}
  static Test() {
    Console.WriteLine("Test2 Initialized");
  }
}
Test.Foo();
Test2.Foo();
```

Self Referencing

C# provides the keywords for accessing the members of a class itself or of the class from which it is derived, namely the `this` and **base** keywords.

this keyword

The `this` keyword denotes a variable that is a reference to a class or struct instance, that is accessible only from within nonstatic function members of the class or struct. The `this` keyword is also used by a constructor to call an overloaded constructor (see the section "Instance

Constructors") or declare or access indexers (see the section "Indexers"). A common use of the `this` variable is to unambiguate a field name from a parameter name:

```
class Dude {
  string name;
  public Test(string name) {
    this.name = name;
  }
  public void Introduce(Dude a) {
    if (a!=this)
      Console.WriteLine("Hello, I'm "+name);
  }
}
```

base keyword

The `base` keyword is similar to the `this` keyword, except that it accesses an overridden or hidden base-class function member. The `base` keyword can also call a base-class constructor (see the section "Instance Constructors") or access a base-class indexer (using `base` instead of `this`). Calling `base` accesses the next most derived class that defines that member. To build upon the example with the `this` keyword:

```
class Hermit : Dude {
  public void new Introduce(Dude a) {
    base.TalkTo(a);
    Console.WriteLine("Nice Talking To You");
  }
}
```

 There is no way to access a specific base class instance member, as with the C++ scope resolution `::` operator.

Destructors and Finalizers

```
attributes?
~class-name ( )
statement-block
```

C# classes can declare destructors. Declaring a C# destructor is simply a syntactic shortcut for declaring a `Finalize` method (known as a finalizer), and is expanded by the compiler into the following method declaration:

```
protected override void Finalize() {
  ...
  base.Finalize();
}
```

Although C# finalizers/destructors appear syntactically similar to C++ destructors, they have vastly different semantics, and it is critical to always be aware of the fact that a C# finalizer/destructor doesn't behave the same as a C++ destructor.

For this reason we recommend that rather than declaring a C# destructor and relying on the compiler to generate a finalizer under the covers, you explicitly declare a **Finalize** method when needed.

Finalizers are class-only methods intended to assist in the cleanup of non-memory resources and are generally called by the garbage collector just before reclaiming unused memory.

For more details on the garbage collector and finalizers, see the section "Automatic Memory Management" in Chapter 3.

Nested Types

A *nested type* is one declared within the scope of another type. Nesting a type has three benefits:

- It can access all the members of its enclosing type, regardless of a member's access modifier.

- It can be hidden from other types with type-member access modifiers.

- Accessing a nested type from outside its enclosing type requires specifying the type name (same principle as static members).

Here's an example of a nested type:

```
using System;
class A {
  int x = 3; // private member
  protected internal class Nested {// choose any access-level
    public void Foo () {
      A a = new A ();
      Console.WriteLine (a.x); //can access A's private members
    }
  }
}
class B {
  static void Main () {
    A.Nested n = new A.Nested (); // Nested is scoped to A
    n.Foo ();
  }
}
```

```
// an example of using "new" on a type declaration
class C : A {
    new public class Nested {} // hide inherited type member
}
```

 Nested classes in C# are roughly equivalent to static inner classes in Java. There is no C# equivalent to Java's nonstatic inner classes, where an inner class has a reference to an instance of the enclosing class.

Interfaces

```
attributes? access-modifier?
new?
interface interface-name [ : base-interface+ ]?
{ interface-members }
```

An interface is like a class, but with these major differences:

- An interface provides a specification rather than an implementation for its members. This is similar to a pure **abstract** class, which is an abstract class consisting of only abstract members.

- A class and struct can implement multiple interfaces; a class can inherit only from a single class.

- A struct can implement an interface; a struct can't inherit from a class.

In the "Classes and Structs" section, we defined polymorphism as the ability to perform the same operations on many types, as long as each type shares a common subset of characteristics. The purpose of an interface is precisely for defining such a set of characteristics.

An interface comprises one or more methods, properties, indexers, and events. These members are always implicitly public and implicitly abstract (therefore virtual and nonstatic).

Defining an Interface

An interface declaration is like a class declaration, but it provides no implementation for its members, since all its members are implicitly abstract. These members are intended to be implemented by a class or struct that implements the interface.

Here's a simple interface that defines a single method:

```
public interface IDelete {
    void Delete();
}
```

Implementing an Interface

Classes or structs that implement an interface may be said to "fulfill the contract of the interface." In this example, GUI controls that support the concept of deleting, such as a `TextBox` or `TreeView`, or your own custom GUI control, can implement the `IDelete` interface:

```
public class TextBox : IDelete {
    public void Delete() {...}
}
public class TreeView : IDelete {
    public void Delete() {...}
}
```

If a class inherits from a base class, the name of each interface to be implemented must appear after the base class name:

```
public class TextBox : Control, IDelete {...}
public class TreeView : Control, IDelete {...}
```

Using an Interface

An interface is useful when you need multiple classes to share characteristics not present in a common base class. In addition, an interface is a good way to ensure that these classes provide their own implementation for the interface member, since interface members are implicitly abstract.

The following example assumes a form containing many GUI controls, including some `TextBox` and `TreeView` controls, where the currently focused control is accessed with the `ActiveControl` property. When a user clicks `Delete` on a menu item or a toolbar button, you test to see if `ActiveControl` implements `IDelete`, and if so, cast it to `IDelete` to call its `Delete` method:

```
class MyForm {
    ...
    void DeleteClick() {
        if (ActiveControl is IDelete) {
            IDelete d = (IDelete)ActiveControl;
            d.Delete();
        }
    }
}
```

Extending an Interface

Interfaces may extend other interfaces. For instance:

```
ISuperDelete : IDelete {
    bool CanDelete {get;}
    event EventHandler CanDeleteChanged;
}
```

In implementing the `ISuperDelete` interface, an `ActiveControl` imple-ments the `CanDelete` property to indicate it has something to delete and isn't read-only. The control also implements the `CanDeleteChanged` event to fire an event whenever its `CanDelete` property changes. This framework lets the application ghost its Delete menu item and toolbar button when the `ActiveControl` is unable to delete.

Explicit Interface Implementation

If there is a name collision between an interface member and an existing member in the class or struct, C# allows you to explicitly implement an interface member to resolve the conflict. In this example, we resolve a conflict that arises when we implement two interfaces that each define a `Delete` method:

```
public interface IDesignTimeControl {
    ...
    object Delete();
}
public class TextBox : IDelete, IDesignTimeControl {
    ...
    void IDelete.Delete() {...}
    object IDesignTimeControl.Delete() {...}
    // Note that explicitly implementing just one of them would
    // be enough to resolve the conflict
}
```

Unlike implicit interface implementations, explicit interface implementa-tions can't be declared with **abstract**, **virtual**, **override**, or **new** modifiers. In addition, they are implicitly **public**, while an implicit imple-mentation requires the use of the **public** modifier. However, to access the method, the class or struct must be cast to the appropriate interface first:

```
TextBox tb = new TextBox();
IDesignTimeControl idtc = (IDesignTimeControl)tb;
IDelete id = (IDelete)tb;
idtc.Delete();
id.Delete();
```

Reimplementing an Interface

If a base class implements an interface member with the `virtual` (or `abstract`) modifier, a derived class can override it. If not, the derived class must reimplement the interface to override that member:

```
public class RichTextBox : TextBox, IDelete {
    // TextBox's IDelete.Delete is not virtual (since explicit
    // interface implementations cannot be virtual)
    public void Delete() {}
}
```

The implementation in this example lets you use a `RichTextBox` object as an `IDelete` object, and to call `RichTextBox`'s version of `Delete`.

Interface Conversions

A class or struct T can be implicitly cast to an interface I that T implements. Similarly, an interface X can be implicitly cast to an interface Y that X inherits from. An interface can be explicitly cast to any other interface or nonsealed class. However, an explicit cast from an interface I to a sealed class or struct T is permitted only if T can implement I. For example:

```
interface IDelete {...}
interface IDesigntimeControl {...}
class TextBox : IDelete, IDesignTimeControl {...}
sealed class Timer : IDesignTimeControl {...}

TextBox tb1 = new TextBox ();
IDelete d = tb1; // implicit cast
IDesignTimeControl dtc = (IDesignTimeControl)d;
TextBox tb2 = (TextBox)dtc;
Timer t = (Timer)d; // illegal, a Timer can never implement IDelete
```

Standard boxing conversions happen when converting between structs and interfaces.

Arrays

```
type [*]+ = new type [ dimension+ ][*]*;
```

Note: [*] is the set: [] [,] [,,] ...

Arrays allow a group of elements of a particular type to be stored in a contiguous block of memory. Array types derive from `System.Array` and are declared in C# using left and right brackets ([]). For instance:

```
char[] vowels = new char[] {'a','e','i','o','u'};
Console.WriteLine(vowels [1]); // Prints "e"
```

The preceding function call prints "e" because array indexes start at 0. To support other languages, .NET can create arrays based on arbitrary start indexes, but the BCL libraries always use zero-based indexing. Once an array has been created, its length can't be changed. However, the System.Collection classes provide dynamically sized arrays, as well as other data structures, such as associative (key/value) arrays (see the section "Collections" in Chapter 3).

Multidimensional Arrays

Multidimensional arrays come in two varieties, rectangular and jagged. *Rectangular* arrays represent an *n*-dimensional block; *jagged* arrays are arrays of arrays:

```
// rectangular
int [,,] matrixR = new int [3, 4, 5]; // creates 1 big cube
// jagged
int [][][] matrixJ = new int [3][][];
int [][][] matrixJ = new int [3][][];
for (int i = 0; i < 3; i++) {
   matrixJ[i] = new int [4][];
   for (int j = 0; j < 4; j++)
      matrixJ[i][j] = new int [5];
}
// assign an element
matrixR [1,1,1] = matrixJ [1][1][1] = 7;
```

Local and Field Array Declarations

For convenience, *local* and *field declarations* can omit the array type when assigning a known value, because the type is specified in the declaration:

```
int[,] array = {{1,2},{3,4}};
```

Array Length and Rank

Arrays know their own length. For multidimensional array methods, the array GetLength method returns the number of elements for a given dimension, which is counted from 0 (the outermost) to the array's Rank-1 (the innermost):

```
// single dimensional
for(int i = 0; i < vowels.Length; i++);
// multi-dimensional
for(int i = 0; i < matrixR.GetLength(2); i++);
```

Bounds Checking

All array indexing is bounds-checked by the CLR, with `IndexOutOf-RangeException` thrown for invalid indexes. As in Java, *bounds checking* prevents program faults and debugging difficulties while enabling code to be executed with security restrictions.

 Generally the performance hit from bounds checking is minor, and the JIT can perform optimizations such as determining each array index is safe before entering a loop, thus avoiding a check made for each iteration. In addition, C# provides unsafe code to explicitly bypass bounds checking (see the section "Unsafe Code and Pointers").

Array Conversions

Arrays of reference types can be converted to other arrays, using the same logic you apply to its element type (this is called *array covariance*). All arrays implement `System.Array`, which provides methods to generically `get` and `set` elements regardless of array type.

Enums

```
attributes? access-modifier?
new?
enum enum-name [ : integer type ]?
{ [attributes? enum-member-name [ = value ]? ]* }
```

Enums specify a group of named numeric constants:

```
public enum Direction {North, East, West, South}
```

Unlike in C, enum members must be used with the enum type name. This resolves naming conflicts and makes code clearer:

```
Direction walls = Direction.East;
```

By default, enums are assigned integer constants 0, 1, 2, etc. You can optionally specify an alternative numeric type to base your enum on and explicitly specify values for each enum member:

```
[Flags]
public enum Direction : byte {
    North=1, East=2, West=4, South=8
}
Direction walls = Direction.North | Direction.West;
```

```
if((walls & Direction.North) != 0)
    System.Console.WriteLine("Can't go north!");
```

The [Flags] attribute is optional. It informs the runtime that the values in the enum can be bit-combined and should be decoded accordingly in the debugger or when outputting text to the console. For example:

```
Console.WriteLine(walls.Format()); // Displays "North|West"
Console.WriteLine(walls); // Calls walls.ToString, displays "5"
```

The System.Enum type also provides many useful static methods for enums that allow you to determine the underlying type of an enum, to check if a specific value is supported, to initialize an enum from a string constant, to retrieve a list of the valid values, and other common operations such as conversions. Here is an example:

```
using System;
public enum Toggle : byte { Off=0, On=1 }
class TestEnum {
  static void Main() {
    Type t = Enum.GetUnderlyingType(typeof(Toggle));
    Console.WriteLine(t); // Prints "Byte"

    bool bDimmed = Enum.IsDefined(typeof(Toggle), "Dimmed");
    Console.WriteLine(bDimmed); // Prints "False"

    Toggle tog =(Switch)Enum.FromString(typeof(Toggle), "On");
    Console.WriteLine(tog); // Prints "1"
    Console.WriteLine(tog.Format()); // Prints "On"

    object[] oa = Enum.GetValues(typeof(Toggle));
    foreach(Toggle tog in oa) // Prints "On=1, Off=0"
      Console.WriteLine("{0}={1}", tog.Format(), tog);
  }
}
```

Enum Operators

The operators relevant to enums are:

==	!=	< >	<=	&
>=	+	-	^	|
-=	+=	=	++	~
sizeof	--			

Enum Conversions

Enums can be explicitly converted to other enums. Enums and numeric types can be explicitly converted to one another. A special case is the numeric literal 0, which can be implicitly converted to an enum.

Delegates

```
attributes? access-modifier?
new?
delegate
[ void | type ]
delegate-name (parameter-list);
```

A *delegate* is a type that defines a method signature, so that delegate instances can hold and invoke a method or list of methods that match its signature. A delegate declaration consists of a name and a method signature. The signature of a delegate method includes its return type and also allows the use of a params modifier in its parameter list, expanding the list of elements that characterize an ordinary method signature. The actual name of the target method is irrelevant to the delegate. Here's an example:

```
delegate bool Filter(string s);
```

This declaration lets you create delegate instances that can hold and invoke methods that return **bool** and have a single string parameter. In the following example a **Filter** is created that holds the **FirstHalf-OfAlphabet** method. You then pass the **Filter** to the **Display** method, which invokes the **Filter**:

```
class Test {
   static void Main() {
      Filter f = new Filter(FirstHalfOfAlphabet);
      Display(new String [] {"Ant","Lion","Yak"}, f);
   }
   static bool FirstHalfOfAlphabet(string s) {
      return "N".CompareTo(s) > 0;
   }
   static void Display(string[] names, Filter f) {
      int count = 0;
      foreach(string s in names)
         if(f(s)) // invoke delegate
            Console.WriteLine("Item {0} is {1}", count++, s);
   }
}
```

Multicast Delegates

If a delegate has a void return type, it is a *multicast* delegate that can hold and invoke multiple methods. In this example, we declare a simple delegate called **MethodInvoker**, which can hold and then invoke the **Foo** and **Goo** methods sequentially. The **+=** method creates a new delegate by adding the right delegate operand to the left delegate operand.

```
delegate void MethodInvoker();
class Test {
    static void Main() {
        new Test(); // prints "Foo","Goo"
    }
    Test() {
        MethodInvoker m = null;
        m += new MethodInvoker(Foo);
        m += new MethodInvoker(Goo);
        m();
    }
    void Foo() {
        Console.WriteLine("Foo");
    }
    void Goo() {
        Console.WriteLine("Goo");
    }
}
```

A delegate can also be removed from another delegate using the -=
operator:

```
Test {
    MethodInvoker m = null;
    m += new MethodInvoker(Foo);
    m -= new MethodInvoker(Foo);
    // m is now null
}
```

Delegates are invoked in the order they are added. Note that the += and
-= operations on a delegate are thread-safe.

To work with the .NET runtime, C# compiles += and -= operations made on a delegate to the static Combine and Remove methods of the System.Delegate class. Delegates with a void return
type alias System.MulticastDelegate. Delegates with a non-
void return type alias (the single-cast) System.Delegate, because
it doesn't make sense to return a value from multiple methods.

Delegates Compared with Function Pointers

A delegate is behaviorally similar to a C function pointer (or Delphi
closure), but delegates can hold multiple methods and hold the instance
associated with each non-static method. In addition, delegates, like all
other C# constructs used outside unsafe blocks, are type-safe and secure,
which means you're protected from pointing to the wrong type of method
or a method that you don't have permission to access.

Delegates Compared with Interfaces

A problem that can be solved with a delegate can also be solved with an interface. For instance, here is how to solve the filter problem using an `IFilter` interface:

```
interface IFilter {
   bool Filter(string s);
}
class Test {
  class FirstHalfOfAlphabetFilter : IFilter {
    public bool Filter(string s) {
      return ("N".CompareTo(s) > 0);
    }
  }
  static void Main() {
    FirstHalfOfAlphabetFilter f = new FirstHalfOfAlphabetFilter();
    Display(new string [] {"Ant", "Lion", "Yak"}, f);
  }
  static void Display(string[] names, IFilter f) {
    int count = 0;
    foreach (string s in names)
      if (f.Filter(s))
        Console.WriteLine("Item {0} is {1}", count++, s);
  }
}
```

In this case, the problem was slightly more elegantly handled with a delegate, but generally delegates are best used for event handling.

Events

Event handling is essentially a process by which one object can notify other objects that an event has occurred. This process is largely encapsulated by multicast delegates, which have this ability built-in.

Defining a Delegate for an Event

The .NET Framework defines many event-handling delegates for you, but you can write your own. For example:

```
delegate void MoveEventHandler(object source, MoveEventArgs e);
```

By convention, an event delegate's first parameter denotes the source of the event, and the delegate's second parameter derives from **System. EventArgs** and stores data about the event.

Storing Data for an Event with EventArgs

The `EventArgs` class can be derived from to include information relevant to a particular event:

```
public class MoveEventArgs : EventArgs {
  public int newPosition;
  public bool cancel;
  public MoveEventArgs(int newPosition) {
    this.newPosition = newPosition;
  }
}
```

Declaring and Firing an Event

A class or struct can declare an event by applying the event modifier to a delegate field. In this example, the `Slider` class has a `Position` property that fires a `Move` event whenever its `Position` changes:

```
class Slider {
  int position;
  public event MoveEventHandler Move;
  public int Position {
    get { return position; }
    set {
      if (position != value) { // if position changed
        if (Move != null) { // if invocation list not empty
          MoveEventArgs args = new MoveEventArgs(value);
          Move(this, args); // fire event
      if (args.cancel)
            return;
        }
        position = value;
      }
    }
  }
}
```

The `event` keyword promotes encapsulation by ensuring that only the `+=` and `-=` operations can be performed on the delegate. This means other classes can register themselves to be notified of the event, but only the `Slider` can invoke the delegate (fire the event) or clear the delegate's invocation list.

Acting on an Event with Event Handlers

You can act on an event by adding an event handler to an event. An *event handler* is a delegate that wraps the method you want invoked when the event is fired.

In the next example, we want our Form to act on changes made to a Slider's Position. You do this by creating a MoveEventHandler delegate that wraps the event-handling method, the slider.Move method. This delegate is added to the Move event's existing list of MoveEventHandlers (which starts off empty). Changing the position on the Slider object fires the Move event, which invokes the slider.Move method:

```
class Form {
  static void Main() {
    Slider slider = new Slider();
    // register with the Move event
    slider.Move += new MoveEventHandler(slider_Move);
    slider.Position = 20;
    slider.Position = 60;
  }
  static void slider_Move(object source, MoveEventArgs e) {
    if(e.newPosition < 50)
      Console.WriteLine("OK");
    else {
      e.cancel = true;
      Console.WriteLine("Can't go that high!");
    }
  }
}
```

Typically the Slider class would be enhanced to fire the Move event whenever its Position is changed by a mouse movement, keypress, or other user action.

 To work with the .NET runtime, an event field adds addOn_XXX and removeOn_XXX methods to the class or struct with stub code that accesses the delegate field that is actually private to the class.

Events as Properties

Event property syntax:

```
attributes? access-modifier?
new? static?
event delegate type event-property-name
 attributes? get statement-block
 attributes? set statement-block
}
```

Although it is convenient to modify a delegate field with the event modifier, it can be inefficient. For instance, a class with 100 events can store

100 delegate fields, even though typically only four of those events are actually assigned. Instead, you can store these delegates in a collection such as a hashtable and use a property rather than a field to expose the event:

```
public event MoveEventHandler Move {
  get {
    return (MoveEventHandler)myEventStorer["Move"];
  }
  set {
    myEventStore ["Move"] = value;
  }
}
```

 Beta 2 event properties use add/remove members.

try Statements and Exceptions

```
try statement-block
[catch(exception type value?)? statement-block]+ |
finally statement-block |
[catch(exception type value?)? statement-block]+
finally statement-block
```

try Statement

The purpose of a **try** statement is to simplify dealing with program execution in exceptional circumstances. A **try** statement does two things. First, it lets exceptions thrown during the **try** block's execution be caught by the **catch** block. Second, it ensures that execution can't leave the **try** block without first executing the **finally** block. A **try** block must be followed by one or more **catch** blocks, a **finally** block, or both.

Exceptions

C# *exceptions* are objects that contain information representing the occurrence of an exceptional program state. When an exceptional state has occurred (e.g., a method receives an illegal value), an exception object may be thrown, and the call-stack is unwound until the exception is caught by an exception handling block. Here's an example:

```
public class File {
  ...
  public static StreamWriter CreateText(string s) {
    ...
    if (!Valid(s))
      throw new IOException("Couldn't create...", ...);
      ...
  }
}
class Test {
  ...
  void Foo(object x) {
    StreamWriter sw = null;
    try {
      sw = File.CreateText("foo.txt");
      sw.Write(x.ToString());
    }
    catch(IOException ex) {
      Console.WriteLine(ex);
    }
    finally {
      if(sw != null)
        sw.Close();
    }
  }
}
```

catch Statement

A **catch** clause specifies what exception type (including derived types) to catch. An exception must be of type **System.Exception**, or a type that derives from **System.Exception**.

Omitting the exception variable

Specifying only an exception type without a variable name allows an exception to be caught when we don't need to use the exception instance, and merely knowing its type will suffice. The example above could have been written like this:

```
catch(IOException) { // don't specify variable
  Console.WriteLine("Couldn't create the foo!");
}
```

Catching System.Exception

To catch any exception at all, a catch clause can omit the **catch** expression. This is just a syntactic shortcut for catching **System.Exception**, since it's the base class for all exceptions.

```
catch {
  Console.WriteLine("Couldn't create the foo!");
}
```

Specifying multiple catch clauses

When declaring multiple `catch` clauses, only the first `catch` clause with an exception type that matches the thrown exception executes its `catch` block. It is illegal for an exception type B to precede an exception type D, if B is a base class of D, since it would be unreachable.

```
try {...}
catch (NullReferenceException) {...}
catch (IOException) {...}
catch {...}
```

finally

`finally` blocks are always executed when control leaves the `try` block. A `finally` block is executed at one of the following times:

- Immediately after the `try` block completes
- Immediately after the `try` block prematurely exits with a jump statement (e.g., `return`, `goto`) and immediately before the target of the jump statement
- Immediately after a `catch` block executes

`finally` blocks are a way to add determinism to a program's execution by ensuring particular code always gets executed.

In our main example, if there is a problem creating *foo.txt*, an `IOException` is thrown that executes the `catch` block, followed by the `finally` block. If x is null, calling `x.ToString()` throws a `NullReferenceException`. The `catch` clause doesn't catch exceptions of this type, but the `finally` block is still executed. This ensures that the file you used is closed before exiting `Foo`.

Key Properties of System.Exception Class

The properties of `System.Exception` you will likely use most frequently include the following:

`StackTrace`
> This is a string representing all the methods called from the origin of the exception to the `catch` block.

`Message`
> This is a string with a description of the error.

InnerException

> Sometimes it is useful to catch an exception, then throw a new, more specific exception. For instance, you can catch an `IOException`, and then throw a `ProblemFooingException`, that contains more specific information on what went wrong. In this scenario, the `ProblemFooingException` should include the IOException as the `InnerException` argument in its constructor, which is assigned to the `InnerException` property. This cascading exception structure can be particularly useful for debugging.

 In C# all exceptions are runtime exceptions; there is no equivalent of Java's compile-time exceptions.

Attributes

> `[[target:]? attribute-name (`
> `positional-param+ |`
> `[named-param = expression]+ |`
> `positional-param+, [named-param = expression]+)?]`

Attributes are language constructs that can decorate a code element (assemblies, modules, types, members, return values, and parameters) with additional information.

In every language, you specify information associated with the types, methods, parameters, and other elements of your program. For example, a type can specify a list of interfaces that it derives from, or a parameter can specify how its values are to be passed with modifiers such as the **ref** modifier in C#. The limitation of this approach is that you can only associate information with code elements using the predefined constructs that the language itself provides.

Attributes allow programmers to add to the types of information associated with these code elements. For example, serialization in the .NET Framework uses various serialization attributes applied to types and fields to define how these code elements are serialized. This is more flexible than requiring the language to have special syntax for serialization.

Attribute Classes

An attribute is defined by a class that inherits (directly or indirectly) from the abstract class **System.Attribute**. When specifying an attribute on an element, the attribute name is the name of the type. By convention the derived type name ends with the word "Attribute", but this suffix isn't required.

In this example we specify that the `Foo` class is serializable using the `Serializable` attribute:

```
[Serializable]
public class Foo {...}
```

The `Serializable` attribute is actually a type declared in the `System` namespace, as follows:

```
class SerializableAttribute : Attribute {...}
```

We could also specify the `Serializable` attribute using its fully qualified typename, as follows:

```
[System.SerializableAttribute]
public class Foo {...}
```

The preceding two examples that use the `Serializable` attribute are semantically identical.

The C# language and the BCL include a number of predefined attributes. For more information on the other attributes included in the BCL, and on creating your own attributes, see the section "Custom Attributes," in Chapter 3.

Named and Positional Parameters

Attributes can take parameters, which specify additional information on the code element beyond the mere presence of the attribute.

In this next example, we specify that the class `Foo` is obsolete using the `Obsolete` attribute. This attribute allows you to include parameters that specify a message and indicate whether the compiler should treat the use of this class as an error:

```
[Obsolete("Use Bar class instead", IsError=true)]
public class Foo {...}
```

Attribute parameters fall into one of two categories: positional and named parameters. In the preceding example, **Use Bar class instead** is a positional parameter, and **IsError=true** is a named parameter.

The positional parameters for an attribute correspond to the parameters passed to one of the attribute type's public constructors. The named parameters for an attribute correspond to the set of public read-write or write-only instance properties and fields on the attribute type.

When specifying an attribute on an element, positional parameters are mandatory, and named parameters are optional.

Since the parameters used when specifying an attribute are evaluated at compile time, they are generally limited to constant expressions.

Attribute Targets

Implicitly, the target of an attribute is the code element it immediately precedes. Sometimes it is necessary to explicitly specify that the attribute applies to a particular target.

In the beta 1 version of the C# compiler, the valid targets are **assembly** and **module**. In future versions of the language, this list of explicit targets is expected to expand to include parameters, return values, etc.

Here is an example that uses the **CLSCompliant** attribute to specify the level of CLS compliance for an entire assembly:

```
[assembly:CLSCompliant(true)]
```

Specifying Multiple Attributes

You can specify multiple attributes on a single code element. Each attribute can be listed within the same pair of square brackets (separated by a comma), in separate pairs of square brackets, or any combination of the two.

Consequently, the following three examples are semantically identical:

```
[Serializable, Obsolete, CLSCompliant(false)]
public class Bar {...}

[Serializable]
[Obsolete]
[CLSCompliant(false)]
public class Bar {...}

[Serializable, Obsolete]
[CLSCompliant(false)]
public class Bar {...}
```

Unsafe Code and Pointers

C# supports direct memory manipulation via pointers within blocks of code marked unsafe. Pointer types are primarily useful for interoperability with C APIs but may also be used for accessing memory outside the managed heap or for performance-critical hotspots.

Pointer Types

For every value type or pointer type V in a C# program, there is a corresponding C# pointer type named V*. A pointer instance holds the address of a value. That value is considered to be of type V, but pointer types can be (unsafely) cast to any other pointer type. Table 2-3 summarizes the principal pointer operators supported by the C# language.

Table 2-3. Principal Pointer Operators

Operator	Meaning
&	The *address-of* operator returns a pointer to the address of a value.
*	The *dereference* operator returns the value at the address of a pointer.
->	The *pointer-to-member* operator is a syntactic shortcut, where x->y is equivalent to (*x).y.

Unsafe Code

Methods, statement blocks, or single statements can be marked with the **unsafe** keyword to perform C++-style pointer operations on memory. Here is an example that uses pointers with a managed object:

```
unsafe void RedFilter(int[,] bitmap) {
  const int length = bitmap.Length;
  fixed (int* b = bitmap) {
    int* p = b;
    for(int i = 0; i < length; i++)
      *p++ &= 0xFF;
  }
}
```

Unsafe code typically runs faster than a corresponding safe implementation, which in this case would have required a nested loop with array indexing and bounds checking. An unsafe C# method can be faster than calling an external C function too, since there is no overhead associated with leaving the managed execution environment.

The fixed Statement

```
fixed ([value type | void ]* name = [&]? expression )
statement-block
```

The **fixed** statement is required to pin a managed object, such as the bitmap in the previous pointer example. During the execution of a program, many objects are allocated and deallocated from the heap. In order to avoid the unnecessary waste or fragmentation of memory, the garbage collector moves objects around. Pointing to an object would be futile if its address can change while referencing it, so the `fixed` statement tells the garbage collector to pin the object and not move it around. This can impact the efficiency of the runtime, so `fixed` blocks should be used only briefly, and preferably heap allocation should be avoided within the `fixed` block.

C# returns a pointer only from a value type, never directly from a reference type. Arrays and strings are an exception to this, but only syntactically, since they actually return a pointer to their first element (which must be a value type), rather than the objects themselves.

Value types declared inline within reference types require the reference type to be pinned, as follows:

```
class Test {
  int x;
  static void Main() {
    Test test = new Test();
    unsafe {
        fixed(int* p = &test.x) { // pins Test
          *p = 9;
        }
        System.Console.WriteLine(test.x);
    }
  }
}
```

Pointer to Member Operator

In addition to the & and * operators, C# also provides the C++-style -> operator, which can be used on structs:

```
struct Test {
  int x;
  unsafe static void Main() {
    Test test = new Test();
    Test* p = &test;
    p->x = 9;
    System.Console.WriteLine(test.x);
  }
}
```

The stackalloc Keyword

Memory can be allocated in a block on the stack explicitly using the `stackalloc` keyword. Since it is allocated on the stack, its lifetime is limited to the execution of the method in which it is used, just as with other local variables. The block may use [] indexing but is purely a value type with no additional self-describing information or bounds checking an array provides;

```
int* a = stackalloc int [10];
for (int i = 0; i < 10; ++i)
   Console.WriteLine(a[i]); // print raw memory
```

Pointers to Unmanaged Code

Pointers are also useful for accessing data outside the managed heap, such as when interacting with C DLLs or COM or when dealing with data not in the main memory, such as graphics memory or a storage medium on an embedded device.

Preprocessor Directives

Preprocessor directives supply the compiler with additional information about regions of code. The most common preprocessor directives are the conditional directives, which provide a way to include or exclude regions of code from compilation. For example:

```
#define DEBUG
class MyClass {
  int x;
  void Foo() {
  # if DEBUG
    Console.WriteLine("Testing: x = {0}", x);
  # endif
  ...
}
```

In this class, the statement in Foo is compiled conditionally, dependent upon the presence of the user-selected DEBUG symbol. If you remove the DEBUG symbol, the statement isn't compiled. Preprocessor symbols can be defined within a source file as just shown, and they can be passed to the compiler with the /define:symbol command-line option. All preprocessor symbols are implicitly true, so the previous #define statement is effectively identical to:

```
#define DEBUG = true
```

The #error and #warning symbols prevent accidental misuse of conditional directives by making the compiler generate a warning or error given an undesirable set of compilation symbols.

Preprocessor Directives

The C# language supports the preprocessor directives shown in Table 2-4.

Table 2-4. Preprocessor Directives

Preprocessor Directive	Action
#define *symbol*	Defines *symbol*
#undef *symbol*	Undefines *symbol*
#if *symbol* [*operator symbol2*] ...	*symbol* to test; *operator*: ==, !=, &&, || followed by #else, #elif, #endif
#else	Executes code to subsequent #endif
#elif *symbol* [*operator symbol2*]	Combines #else branch and #if test
#endif	Ends conditional directives
#warning *text*	*text*: warning text to appear in compiler output
#error *text*	*text*: error manager to appear in compiler output
#line *number* [*file*]	*number* specifies line in source code; *file* is the filename to appear in computer output
#region *name*	Marks beginning of outline
#end *region*	Ends an outline region

XML Documentation

C# offers three different styles of source-code documentation: single-line comments, multiline comments, and documentation comments.

C/C++-Style Comments

Single- and multiline comments use the C++ syntax: // and /*...*/:

```
int x = 3; // this is a comment
MyMethod(); /* this is a
comment that spans two lines */
```

The disadvantage of this style of commenting is that there is no predetermined standard for documenting your types. Consequently, it can't be easily parsed to automate the production of documentation. C# improves on this by allowing you to embed documentation comments in the source, and by providing an automated mechanism for extracting and validating documentation at compile time.

Documentation Comments

Documentation comments are similar to C# single-line comments but start with /// and can be applied to any user-defined type or member. These comments can include embedded XML tags as well as descriptive text. These tags allow you to mark up the descriptive text to better define the semantics of the type or member and also to incorporate cross-references.

These comments can then be extracted at compile time into a separate output file containing the documentation. The compiler validates the comments for internal consistency, expands cross references into fully qualified type IDs, and outputs a well-formed XML file. Further processing is left up to you, although a common next step is to run the XML through an XSL/T, generating HTML documentation.

Here is an example documentation for a simple type:

```
// Filename: DocTest.cs
using System;
class MyClass {
   /// <summary>
   /// The Foo method is called from
   ///    <see cref="Main">Main</see>
   /// </summary>
   /// <mytag>Secret stuff</mytag>
   /// <param name="s">Description for s</param>
   static void Foo(string s) { Console.WriteLine(s); }
   static void Main() { Foo("42"); }
}
```

XML Documentation Files

When the preceding source file is run through the compiler with the /doc:*<filename>* command-line options, this XML file is generated:

```
<?xml version="1.0"?>
<doc>
   <assembly>
      <name>DocTest</name>
   </assembly>
   <members>
      <member name="M:MyClass.Foo(System.String)">
         <summary>
         The Foo method is called from
            <see cref="M:MyClass.Main">Main</see>
         </summary>
         <mytag>Secret stuff</mytag>
         <param name="s">Description for s</param>
      </member>
   </members>
</doc>
```

The <?xml...>, <doc>, and <members> tags are generated automatically and form the skeleton for the XML file. The <assembly> and <name> tags indicate the assembly that this type lives in. Every member preceded by a documentation comment is included in the XML file via a <member> tag with a name attribute that identifies the member. Note that the `cref` attribute in the `<see>` tag has also been expanded to refer to a fully qualified type and member. The predefined XML documentation tags embedded in the documentation comments are also included in the XML file. The tags have been validated to ensure that all parameters are documented, that the names are accurate, and that any cross references to other types or members can be resolved. Finally, any additional user-defined tags are transferred verbatim.

Predefined XML Tags

This section lists the predefined set of XML tags that can be used to mark up the descriptive text:

`<summary>`, `<remarks>`

```
<summary>description</summary>
<remarks>description</remarks>
```

These tags describe a type or member. Typically, `<summary>` contains a brief overview, and `<remarks>` contains a full description.

`<param>`

```
<param name= "name">description</param>
```

This tag describes a parameter on a method. The *name* attribute is mandatory and must refer to a parameter on the method. If this tag is applied to any parameter on a method, all parameters on that method must be documented. You must enclose *name* in double quotation marks (`""`).

`<returns>`

```
<returns>description</returns>
```

This tag describes the return values for a method.

`<exception>`

```
<exception [cref= "type"]>description</exception>
```

This tag describes the exceptions a method may throw. If present, the optional `cref` attribute should refer to the type of the exception. You must enclose the type name in double quotation marks (`""`).

`<permission>`

```
<permission [cref="type"]>description</permission>
```

This tag describes the permission requirements for a type or member. If present, the optional `cref` attribute should refer to the type that represents the permission set required by the member, although the compiler doesn't validate this. You must enclose the type name in double quotation marks (`""`).

<example>, <c>, <code>

```
<example>description</example>
<c>code</c>
<code>code</code>
```

These tags provide a description and sample source code explaining the use of a type or member. Typically the `<example>` tag provides the description and contains the `<c>` and `<code>` tags, although these can also be used independently. If you need to include an inline code snippet, use the `<c>` tag. If you need to include multiline snippets, use the `<code>` tag.

<see>, <seealso>

```
<see cref="member">text</see>
<seealso cref="member">text</seealso>
```

These tags identify cross references in the documentation to other types or members. Typically, the `<see>` tag is used inline within a description, while the `<seealso>` tag is broken out into a separate "See Also" section. These tags are useful because they allow tools to generate cross references, indexes, and hyperlinked views of the documentation. Member names must be enclosed by double quotation marks (`""`).

<value>

```
<value>description</value>
```

This tag describes a property on a class.

<paramref>

```
<paramref name="name" />
```

This tag identifies the use of a parameter name. The name must be enclosed by double quotation marks (`""`).

<list>, <para>

```
<list type=[bullet|number|table]>
 <listheader>
 <term>name</term>
 <description>description</description>
 </listheader>
 <item>
 <term>name</term>
 <description>description</description>
 </item>
</list>
<para>text</para>
```

These tags provide hints to documentation generators on how to format the documentation.

User-Defined Tags

There is little that is special about the predefined XML tags recognized by the C# compiler, and you are free to define your own. The only special processing done by the compiler is on the <param> tag (where it verifies the parameter name and confirms that all the parameters on the method are documented) and the cref attribute (where it verifies that the attribute refers to a real type or member, and expands it to a fully qualified type or member ID). The cref attribute can also be used in your own tags and is verified and expanded just as it is in the predefined <exception>, <permission>, <see>, and <seealso> tags.

Type or Member Cross References

Type names and type or member cross references are translated into IDs that uniquely define the type or member. These names are composed of a prefix that defines what the ID represents and a signature of the type or member. Table 2-5 lists the set of type and member prefixes.

Table 2-5. XML Type ID Prefixes

Prefix	Applied to
N	Namespace
T	Type (class, struct, enum, interface, delegate)
F	Field
P	Property (includes indexers)
M	Method (includes special methods)
E	Event
!	Error

The rules describing how the signatures are generated are well documented, although fairly complex.

Here is an example of a type and the IDs that are generated:

```
// Namespaces do not have independent signatures
namespace NS {
  // T:NS.MyClass
  class MyClass {
    // F:NS.MyClass.aField
    string aField;
    // P:NS.MyClass.aProperty
    short aProperty {get {...} set {...}}
    // T:NS.MyClass.NestedType
    class NestedType {...};
    // M:NS.MyClass.X()
    void X() {...}
```

```
    // M:NS.MyClass.Y(System.Int32,System.Double@,System.Decimal@)
    void Y(int p1, ref double p2, out decimal p3) {...}
    // M:NS.MyClass.Z(System.Char[],System.Single[0:,0:])
    void Z(char[] p1, float[,] p2) {...}
    // M:NS.MyClass.op_Addition(NS.MyClass,NS.MyClass)
    public static MyClass operator+(MyClass c1, MyClass c2) {...}
    // M:NS.MyClass.op_Implicit(NS.MyClass)~System.Int32
    public static implicit operator int(MyClass c) {...}
    // M:NS.MyClass.#ctor
    MyClass() {...}
    // M:NS.MyClass.Finalize
    ~MyClass() {...}
    // M:NS.MyClass.#cctor
    static MyClass() {...}
  }
}
```

3

Programming the .NET Framework

Most modern programming languages include some form of runtime that provides common services and access to the underlying operating systems and hardware. Examples of this range from a simple functional library, such as the ANSI C Runtime used by C and C++, to the rich object-oriented class libraries provided by the Java Runtime Environment.

Similar to the way that Java programs depend on the Java class libraries and virtual machine, C# programs depend on the services in the .NET Framework such as the base class libraries (BCL) and the Common Language Runtime (CLR).

For a high-level overview of the BCL, see Chapter 4, *Base Class Library Overview*.

This chapter addresses the most common tasks you need to perform when building C# programs. These topics generally fall into one of two categories: leveraging functionality included in the BCL and interacting with elements of the CLR.

Common Types

Certain types in the BCL are ubiquitous, in that they are fundamental to the way the BCL and CLR work and provide common functionality used throughout the entire BCL.

This section identifies some of the most common of these types and provides guidelines on their usage. The types mentioned in this section all exist in the System namespace.

Object Class

The System.Object class is the root of the class hierarchy and serves as the base class for every other class. The C# object type aliases System.Object. System.Object provides a handful of useful methods that are present on all objects, and whose signatures are listed in the following fragment of the System.Object class definition:

```
public class Object {
    public Object() {...}
    public virtual bool Equals(object o) {...}
    public virtual int GetHashCode(){...}
    public Type GetType(){...}
    public virtual string ToString() {...}
    protected virtual void Finalize() {...}
    protected object MemberwiseClone() {...}
}
```

Object(object o)

The constructor for the Object base class.

Equals()

This method evaluates whether two objects are equivalent.

The default implementation of this method compares the objects by reference, so classes are expected to override this method to compare two objects by value.

In C#, you can also override the == and != operators. For more information see "Implementing value equality" in the "Classes and Structs" section in Chapter 2, *C# Language Reference*.

GetHashCode()

This method allows objects to provide their own hash function for use in collections.

The return value from this function should pass the following tests: (1) two objects representing the same value should return the same hashcode, and (2) the returned values should generate a random distribution at runtime.

The default implementation of GetHashCode actually doesn't meet these criteria, as it merely returns a number based on the object reference. For this reason, you should usually override this method in your own types.

To learn more about how the hashcode is used by the predefined collection classes, see "Collections," later in this chapter.

GetType()

> This method provides access to the **Type** object representing the type of the object, and should never be implemented by your types. To learn more about the **Type** object and reflection in general, see the later section "Reflection."

ToString()

> This method provides a string representation of the object and is generally intended for use when debugging.

> The default implementation of this method merely returns the name of the type and should be overridden in your own types to return a meaningful string representation of the object. The predefined types such as int and string, all override this method to return the value, as follows:

```
using System;
class Beeblebrox {}
class Test {
  static void Main() {
    string s = "Zaphod";
    Beeblebrox b = new Beeblebrox();
    Console.WriteLine(s); // Prints "Zaphod"
    Console.WriteLine(b); // Prints "Beeblebrox"
  }
}
```

Finalize()

> The **Finalize** method cleans up nonmemory resources and is usually called by the garbage collector before reclaiming the memory for the object. The **Finalize** method can be overridden on any reference type, but this should be done only in a very few cases. For a discussion of finalizers and the garbage collector, see the later section "Automatic Memory Management."

MemberwiseClone()

> This method creates shallow copies of the object and should never be implemented by your types. To learn how to control shallow/deep copy semantics on your own types, see the upcoming section "ICloneable Interface."

Creating BCL-friendly types

When defining new types that work well with the rest of the BCL, you should override several of these methods as appropriate. Some of these overrides have parallels with C# operators that can also be overridden where it makes sense.

Here is an example of a new value type that is intended to be a good citizen in the BCL:

```
public class Point3D {
  public int x, y, z;
  public Point3D(int x, int y, int z) {
    this.x=x; this.y=y; this.z=z; // Initialize data
  }
  public override bool Equals(object o) {
    if (!(o is Point3D)) // Check for type equivalence
      return false;
    return (this==(Point3D)o); // Implemented by operator==
  }
  public static bool operator !=(Point3D lhs, Point3D rhs) {
    return (!(lhs==rhs)); // Implemented by operator==
  }
  public static bool operator ==(Point3D lhs, Point3D rhs) {
    return ((rhs.x==lhs.x) && (rhs.y==lhs.y) && (rhs.z==lhs.z));
  }
  public override int GetHashCode(){
    return x^y^z;
  }
  public override string ToString() {
    return String.Format("[{0},{1},{2}]", x, y, z);
  }
}
```

This class overrides **Equals**, **operator==**, and **operator!=** to provide value-based equality semantics, creates a hashcode that follows the rules described in the preceding section, and overrides **ToString** for easy debugging. It can be used as follows:

```
using System;
using System.Collections;
public class Point3D {...}
class TestPoint3D {
  static void Main() {
    // Uses ToString, prints "p1=[1,1,1] p2=[2,2,2] p3=[2,2,2]"
    Point3D p1 = new Point3D(1,1,1);
    Point3D p2 = new Point3D(2,2,2);
    Point3D p3 = new Point3D(2,2,2);
    Console.WriteLine("p1={0} p2={1} p3={2}", p1, p2, p3);

    // Tests for equality to demonstrate Equals, == & !=
    int i = 100;
    Console.WriteLine(p1.Equals(i)); // Prints "False"
    Console.WriteLine(p1==p2); // Prints "False"
    Console.WriteLine(p2==p3); // Prints "True"

    // Use a hashtable to store points (uses GetHashCode)
    Hashtable ht = new Hashtable();
    ht["p1"] = p1;
    ht["p2"] = p2;
    ht["p3"] = p3;
```

```
    // Prints "p2=[2,2,2] p3=[2,2,2] p1=[1,1,1]"
    foreach (DictionaryEntry de in ht)
      Console.Write("{0}={1} ", de.Key, de.Value);
  }
}
```

ICloneable Interface

```
public interface ICloneable {
  object Clone();
}
```

ICloneable allows classes or structs instances to be cloned. It contains a single method named Clone that returns a copy of the instance. When implementing this interface your Clone method can either simply return **this.MemberwiseClone()**, which performs a shallow copy (the fields are copied directly), or you can perform a custom deep copy, where you clone individual fields in the class or struct. The following example is the simplest implementation **ICloneable**:

```
public class Foo : ICloneable {
    public object Clone() {
      return this.MemberwiseClone();
  }
}
```

IComparable Interface

```
interface IComparable {
  int CompareTo(object o);
}
```

IComparable is implemented by types that have instances that can be ordered (see the later section "Collections"). It contains a single method named **CompareTo** that:

- Returns - if instance < o

- Returns + if instance > o

- Returns 0 if instance == o

This interface is implemented by all numeric types, **string**, **DateTime**, etc. It may also be implemented by custom classes or structs to provide comparison semantics. For example:

```
using System;
using System.Collections;
class MyType : IComparable {
  public int x;
  public MyType(int x) {
    this.x = x;
  }
```

```
    public int CompareTo(object o) {
      return x -((MyType)o).x;
    }
  }
  class Test {
    static void Main() {
      ArrayList a = new ArrayList();
      a.Add(new MyType(42));
      a.Add(new MyType(17));
      a.Sort();
      foreach(MyType t in a)
        Console.WriteLine(((MyType)t).x);
    }
  }
```

IFormattable Interface

```
public interface IFormattable {
  string Format(string format, IServiceObjectProvider sop);
}
```

The IFormattable interface is implemented by types that have formatting options for converting their value to a string representation. For instance, a decimal may be converted to a string representing currency, or a string which uses a comma for a decimal point. The formatting options are specified by the *format string* (see the section "Formatting Strings"). If an IServiceObjectProvider interface is supplied, it specifies the specific culture to be used for the conversion.

IFormattable is commonly used when calling one of the String class Format methods (see the laster section "Strings").

All the common types (int, string, DateTime, etc.) implement this interface, and you should implement it on your own types if you want them to be fully supported by the String class when formatting.

Math

C# and the BCL provide a rich set of features that make math-oriented programming easy and efficient.

This section identifies some of the most common types applicable to math programming and demonstrates how to build new math types. The types mentioned in this section exist in the System namespace.

Language Support for Math

C# has many useful features for math, and can even build custom mathematical types. Operator overloading allows custom mathematical types,

such as complex numbers and vectors, to be used in a natural way. Rectangular arrays provide a fast and easy way to express matrices. Finally,
structs allow the efficient creation of low-overhead objects. For example:

```
struct Vector {
  float direction;
  float magnitude;
  public Vector(float direction, float magnitude) {
    this.direction = direction;
    this.magnitude = magnitude;
  }
  public static Vector operator *(Vector v, float scale) {
    return new Vector(v.direction, v.magnitude * scale);
  }
  public static Vector operator /(Vector v, float scale) {
    return new Vector(v.direction, v.magnitude * scale);
  }
  ...
}
class Test {
  static void Main() {
  Vector [,] matrix = {{new Vector(1f,2f), new Vector(6f,2f)},
                       {new Vector(7f,3f), new Vector(4f,9f)}};
  for (int i=0; i<matrix.GetLength(0); i++)
    for (int j=0; j<matrix.GetLength(1); j++)
      matrix[i, j] *= 2f;
  }
```

Special Types and Operators

The **decimal** datatype is useful for financial calculations, since it is a
base$_{10}$ number that can store 28 to 29 significant figures (see "decimal
type" in the "Types" section in Chapter 2).

The **checked** operator allows integral operations to be bounds checked
(see "Arithmetic Overflow Check Operators" in the "Expressions and
Operators" section in Chapter 2).

Math Class

The **Math** class provides static methods and constants for basic mathematical purposes. All trigonometric and exponential functions use the **double**
type, and all angles use radians. For example:

```
using System;
class Test {
  static void Main() {
    double a = 3;
    double b = 4;
    double C = Math.PI / 2;
    double c = Math.Sqrt (a*a+b*b-2*a*b*Math.Cos(C));
```

```
        Console.WriteLine("The length of side c is "+c);
    }
}
```

Random Class

The `Random` class produces pseudo-random numbers and may be extended if you require greater randomness. The random values returned are always between a minimum (inclusive) value and a maximum (exclusive) value. By default, the `Random` class uses the current time as its seed, but a custom seed can also be supplied to the constructor. Here's a simple example:

```
Random r = new Random();
Console.WriteLine(r.Next(50)); // return between 0 and 50
```

Strings

C# offers a wide range of string-handling features. Support is provided for both mutable and immutable strings, extensible string formatting, locale-aware string comparisons, and multiple string encoding systems.

This section introduces and demonstrates the most common types you'll use in working with strings. Unless otherwise stated, the types mentioned in this section all exist in the `System` or `System.Text` namespaces.

String Class

A C# string represents an immutable sequence of characters, and aliases the `System.String` class. Strings have comparison, appending, inserting, conversion, copying, formatting, indexing, joining, splitting, padding, trimming, removing, replacing, and searching methods. The compiler converts + operations on operands where the left operand is a string to `Concat` methods and preevaluates and interns string constants where possible.

Immutability of Strings

Strings are immutable, which means they can't be modified after creation. Consequently, many of the methods that initially appear to modify a string actually create a new string:

```
string a = "Heat";
string b = a.Insert(3, "r");
Console.WriteLine(b); // Prints Heart
```

If you need a mutable string, see the `StringBuilder` class.

String Interning

In addition, the immutability of strings enable all strings in an application to be interned. *Interning* describes the process whereby all the constant strings in an application are stored in a common place, and any duplicate strings are eliminated. This saves space at runtime but creates the possibility that multiple string references will point at the same spot in memory. This can be the source of unexpected results when comparing two constant strings, as follows:

```
string a = "hello";
string b = "hello";
Console.WriteLine(a == b); // True for String only
Console.WriteLine(a.Equals(b)); // True for all objects
Console.WriteLine((object)a == (object)b); // True!!
```

Formatting Strings

The `Format` method provides a convenient way to build strings that embed string representations of a variable number of parameters. Each parameter can be of any type, including both predefined types and user-defined type.

The `Format` method takes a format-specification string and a variable number of parameters. The format-specification string defines the template for the string and includes format specifications for each of the parameters. The syntax of a format specifier looks like this:

```
{ParamIndex[,MinWidth][:FormatString]}
```

`ParamIndex`
The zero-based index of the parameter to be formatted.

`MinWidth`
The minimum number of characters for the string representation of the parameter, to be padded by spaces if necessary (negative is left-justified, positive is right-justified).

`FormatString`
If the parameter represents an object that implements `IFormattable`, the `FormatString` is passed to the `Format` method on `IFormattable` to construct the string. If not, the `ToString` method on `Object` is used to construct the string.

All of the common types (`int`, `string`, `DateTime`, etc.) implement `IFormattable`. A table of the numeric and picture format specifiers supported by the common predefined types is provided in Appendix C, *Format Specifiers*.

In the following example, we embed a basic string representation of the account variable (param 0), and a monetary string representation of the cash variable (param 1, C=Currency):

```
using System;
class TestFormatting {
  static void Main() {
    int i = 2;
    decimal m = 42.73m;
    string s = String.Format("Account {0} has {1:C}.", i, m);
    Console.WriteLine(s); // Prints "Account 2 has $42.73"
  }
}
```

Indexing Strings

Consistent with all other indexing in the CLR, the characters in a string are accessed with a zero-based index:

```
using System;
class TestIndexing {
  static void Main() {
    string s = "Going down?";
    for (int i=0; i<s.Length; i++)
      Console.WriteLine(s[i]); // Prints s vertically
  }
}
```

Encoding Strings

Strings can be converted between different character encodings using the `Encoding` type. The `Encoding` type can't be created directly, but the ASCII, Unicode, UTF7, UTF8, and `BigEndianUnicode` static properties on the `Encoding` type return correctly constructed instances.

Here is an example that converts an array of bytes into a string using the ASCII encoding:

```
using System;
using System.Text;
class TestEncoding {
  static void Main() {
    byte[] ba = new byte[] { 67, 35, 32, 105, 115,
                             32, 67, 79, 79, 76, 33 };
```

```
        string s = Encoding.ASCII.GetString(ba);
        Console.WriteLine(s);
    }
}
```

StringBuilder Class

The `StringBuilder` class is used to represent mutable strings. It starts at a predefined size (16 characters by default) and grows dynamically as more string data is added. It can either grow unbounded or up to a configurable maximum. For example:

```
using System;
using System.Text;
class TestStringBuilder {
    static void Main() {
        StringBuilder sb = new StringBuilder("Hello, ");
        sb.Append("World");
        sb[11] = '!';
        Console.WriteLine(sb); // Hello, World!
    }
}
```

Collections

Collections are standard data structures that supplement arrays, the only built-in data structures in C#. This differs from languages such as Perl and Python, which incorporate key-value data structures and dynamically sized arrays into the language itself.

The BCL includes a set of types that provide commonly required data structures and support for creating your own. These types are typically broken down into two categories: *interfaces* that define a standardized set of design patterns for collection classes in general, and concrete *classes* that implement these interfaces and provide a usable range of data structures.

This section introduces all the concrete collection classes and abstract collection interfaces and provides examples of their use. Unless otherwise stated, the types mentioned in this section all exist in the `System.Collections` namespace.

Concrete Collection Classes

The BCL includes the concrete implementations of the collection design patterns that are described in this section.

Unlike C++, C# doesn't yet support templates, so these implementations work generically by accepting elements of type `System.Object`.

ArrayList class

`ArrayList` is a dynamically sized array of objects that implements the `IList` interface (see the upcoming section "IList interface"). An `Array-List` works by maintaining an internal array of objects that is replaced with a larger array when it reaches its capacity of elements. It is very efficient at adding elements (since there is usually a free slot at the end) but is inefficient at inserting elements (since all elements have to be shifted to make a free slot). Searching can be efficient if the `BinarySearch` method is used on an `ArrayList` that has been sorted but is otherwise inefficient (and requires each item be checked).

```
ArrayList a = new ArrayList();
a.Add("Vernon");
a.Add("Corey");
a.Add("William");
a.Add("Muzz");
a.Sort();
for(int i = 0; i < a.Count; i++)
   Console.WriteLine(a [i]);
```

BitArray class

A `BitArray` is a dynamically sized array of Boolean values. It is more memory-efficient than a simple array of `bool`s, because it uses only one bit for each value, whereas a `bool` array uses two bytes for each value. Here is an example of its use:

```
BitArray bits = new BitArray();
bits.Length = 2;
bits[1] = true;
bits.Xor(bits); // Xor the array with itself
```

Hashtable class

A `Hashtable` is a standard dictionary (key/value) data structure that uses a hashing algorithm to store and index values efficiently. This hashing algorithm is performed using the hashcode returned by the `GetHashCode` method on `System.Object`. Types stored in a `Hashtable` should therefore override `GetHashCode` to return a good hash of the object's internal value.

```
Hashtable ht = new Hashtable();
ht["One"] = 1;
ht["Two"] = 2;
ht["Three"] = 3;
Console.WriteLine(ht["Two"]); // Prints "2"
```

Hashtable also implements **IDictionary** (see the section "IDictionary interface"), and therefore can be manipulated as a normal dictionary data structure.

Queue class

A **Queue** is a standard first-in first-out (FIFO) data structure, providing simple operations to enqueue, dequeue, peek, etc. Here is an example:

```
Queue q = new Queue();
q.Enqueue(1);
q.Enqueue(2);
Console.WriteLine(q.Dequeue()); // Prints "1"
Console.WriteLine(q.Dequeue()); // Prints "2"
```

SortedList class

A **SortedList** is a standard dictionary data structure that uses a binary-chop search to index efficiently. **SortedList** implements **IDictionary** (see the section "IDictionary interface"):

```
SortedList s = new SortedList();
s["Zebra"] = 1;
s["Antelope"] = 2;
s["Eland"] = 3;
s["Giraffe"] = 4;
s["Meerkat"] = 5;
s["Dassie"] = 6;
s["Tokoloshe"] = 7;
Console.WriteLine(s["Meerkat"]); // Prints "5" in 3 lookups
```

Stack class

A **Stack** is a standard last-in first-out (LIFO) data structure:

```
Stack s = new Stack();
s.Push(1); // Stack = 1
s.Push(2); // Stack = 1,2
s.Push(3); // Stack = 1,2,3
Console.WriteLine(s.Pop()); // Prints 3, Stack=1,2
Console.WriteLine(s.Pop()); // Prints 2, Stack=1
Console.WriteLine(s.Pop()); // Prints 1, Stack=
```

StringCollection class

A **StringCollection** is a standard collection data structure for storing strings. **StringCollection** implements **ICollection** and can be manipulated like a normal collection (see the section "ICollection interface"):

```
StringCollection sc = new StringCollection();
sc.Add("s1");
string[] sarr = {"s2", "s3", "s4"};
sc.AddRange(sarr);
```

```
foreach (string s in sc)
  Console.Write("{0} ", s); // s1 s2 s3 s4
```

Collection Interfaces

The collection interfaces provide standard ways to enumerate, populate, and author collections. The BCL defines the interfaces in this section to support the standard collection design patterns.

IEnumerable interface

```
public interface IEnumerable {
  IEnumerator GetEnumerator();
}
```

The C# **foreach** statement works on any collection that implements the **IEnumerable** interface. The **IEnumerable** interface has a single method that returns an **IEnumerator** object.

IEnumerator interface

```
public interface IEnumerator {
  bool MoveNext();
  object Current {get;}
  void Reset();
}
```

The **IEnumerator** interface provides a standard way to iterate over collections. Internally, an **IEnumerator** maintains the current position of an item in the collection. If the items are numbered 0 (inclusive) to n (exclusive), the current position starts off as -1, and finishes at n.

IEnumerator is typically implemented as a nested type and is initialized by passing the collection to the constructor of the **IEnumerator**:

```
using System.Collections;
public class MyCollection : IEnumerable {
  // ...
  public virtual IEnumerator GetEnumerator () {
    return new MyCollection.Enumerator(this);
  }
  private class Enumerator : IEnumerator {
    private MyCollection collection;
    private int currentIndex = -1;

    internal Enumerator (MyCollection collection) {
      this.collection = collection;
    }
    public object Current {
      get {
        if (currentIndex == collection.Count)
          throw new InvalidOperationException();
        return collection [currentIndex];
```

```
      }
    }
    public bool MoveNext () {
      if (currentIndex > collection.Count)
        throw new InvalidOperationException();
      return ++currentIndex < collection.Count;
    }
    public void Reset () {
      currentIndex = -1;
    }
  }
}
```

The collection can then be enumerated in either of these two ways:

```
MyCollection mcoll = new MyCollection();
...
// Using foreach: substitute your typename for XXX
foreach (XXX item in mcoll) {
  Console.WriteLine(item);
  ...
}
// Using IEnumerator: substitute your typename for XXX
IEnumerator ie = myc.GetEnumerator();
while (myc.MoveNext()) {
  XXX item = (XXX)myc.Current;
  Console.WriteLine(item);
  ...
}
```

ICollection interface

```
public interface ICollection : IEnumerable {
  void CopyTo(Array array, int index);
  int Count {get;}
  bool IsReadOnly {get;}
  bool IsSynchronized {get;}
  object SyncRoot {get;}
}
```

`ICollection` is the interface implemented by all collections, including arrays, and provides the following methods:

`CopyTo(Array array, int index)`
   This method copies all the elements into the array starting at the specified index.

`Count`
   This property returns the number of elements in the collection.

`IsReadOnly`
   This property returns if a collection can be modified.

`IsSynchronized()`

> This method allows you to determine whether a collection is thread-safe. The collections provided in the BCL are not themselves thread-safe, but each one includes a `Synchronized` method that returns a thread-safe wrapper of the collection.

`SyncRoot()`

> This property returns an object (usually the collection itself) that can be locked to provide basic thread-safe support for the collection.

IComparer interface

```
public interface IComparer {
    int Compare(object x, object y);
}
```

`IComparer` is a standard interface that compares two objects for sorting in `Array`s. You generally don't need to implement this interface, since a default implementation that uses the `IComparable` interface is already provided by the `Comparer` type, which is used by the `Array` type.

IList interface

```
public interface IList : ICollection, IEnumerable {
    object this [int index] {get; set}
    int Add(object o);
    void Clear();
    bool Contains(object value);
    int IndexOf(object value);
    void Insert(int index, object value);
    void Remove(object value);
    void RemoveAt(int index);
}
```

`IList` is an interface for array-indexable collections, such as `ArrayList`.

IDictionary interface

```
public interface IDictionary : ICollection, IEnumerable {
    object this [object key] {get; set};
    ICollection Keys {get;}
    ICollection Values {get;}
    void Clear();
    bool Contains(object value);
    IDictionaryEnumerator GetEnumerator();
    void Remove(object key);
}
```

`IDictionary` is an interface for key/value-based collections, such as `Hashtable` and `SortedList`.

IDictionaryEnumerator interface

```
public interface IDictionaryEnumerator : IEnumerator {
   DictionaryEntry Entry {get;}
   object Key {get;}
   object Value {get;}
}
```

`IDictionaryEnumerator` is a standardized interface that enumerates over the contents of a dictionary.

IHashCodeProvider interface

```
public interface IHashCodeProvider {
   int GetHashCode(object o);
}
```

`IHashCodeProvider` is a standard interface used by the `Hashtable` collection to hash its objects for storage.

Regular Expressions

The BCL includes support for performing regular expression matching and replacement capabilities. The expressions are based on Perl5 *regexp*, including lazy quantifiers (`??`, `*?`, `+?`, `{n,m}?`), positive and negative lookahead, and conditional evaluation.

The types mentioned in this section all exist in the `System.Text.RegularExpressions` namespace.

Regex Class

The `Regex` class is the heart of the BCL regular expression support. Used both as an object instance and a static type, the `Regex` class represents an immutable, compiled instance of a regular expression that can be applied to a string via a matching process.

Internally, the regular expression is stored as either a sequence of internal regular expression bytecodes that are interpreted at match time or as compiled MSIL opcodes that are JIT-compiled by the CLR at runtime. This allows you to make a tradeoff between worsened regular expression startup time and memory utilization versus higher raw match performance at runtime.

For more information on the regular-expression options, supported character escapes, substitution patterns, character sets, positioning assertions, quantifiers, grouping constructs, backreferences, and alternation, see Appendix B, *Regular Expressions*.

Match and MatchCollection Classes

The `Match` class represents the result of applying a regular expression to a string, looking for the first successful match. The `MatchCollection` class contains a collection of `Match` instances that represent the result of applying a regular expression to a string recursively until the first unsuccessful match occurs.

Group Class

The `Group` class represents the results from a single grouping expression. From this class, it is possible to drill down to the individual subexpression matches with the `Captures` property.

Capture and Capture Collection Classes

The `CaptureCollection` class contains a collection of `Capture` instances, each representing the results of a single subexpression match.

Using Regular Expressions

Combining these classes, you can create the following example:

```
/*
 * Sample showing multiple groups,
 * and groups with multiple captures
 * Build the sample as:
 * csc /r:System.Text.RegularExpressions.dll test.cs
 */
using System;
using System.Text.RegularExpressions;
class Test
  {
  static void Main()
    {
    string text = "abracadabra1abracadabra2abracadabra3";
    string pat = @"
    (          # start the first group
      abra  # match the literal 'abra'
      (          # start the second (inner) group
      cad    # match the literal 'cad'
      )?      # end the second (optional) group
    )          # end the first group
    +          # match one or more occurences
    ";
    Console.WriteLine("Original text = ["+text+"]");
    Regex r = new Regex(pat, "x");// use 'x' modifier to ignore comments
    int[] gnums = r.GetGroupNumbers();// get the list of group numbers
    Match m = r.Match(text);// get first match
    while (m.Success)
```

```
    {
    for (int i = 1; i < gnums.Length; i++)// start at group 1
  {
  Group g = m.Group(gnums[i]);// get the group for this match
  Console.WriteLine("Group"+gnums[i]+"=["+g.ToString()+"]");
  CaptureCollection cc = g.Captures;// get caps for this group
  for (int j = 0; j < cc.Count; j++)
    {
    Capture c = cc[j];
    Console.WriteLine("Capture" + j + "=["+c.ToString() +
              "] Index=" + c.Index + " Length=" + c.Length);
    }
  }
    m = m.NextMatch();// get next match
    }
  }
}
```

The preceding example produces the following output:

```
Original text = [abracadabra1abracadabra2abracadabra3]
Group1=[abra]
    Capture0=[abracad] Index=0 Length=7
    Capture1=[abra] Index=7 Length=4
Group2=[cad]
    Capture0=[cad] Index=4 Length=3
Group1=[abra]
    Capture0=[abracad] Index=12 Length=7
    Capture1=[abra] Index=19 Length=4
Group2=[cad]
    Capture0=[cad] Index=16 Length=3
Group1=[abra]
    Capture0=[abracad] Index=24 Length=7
    Capture1=[abra] Index=31 Length=4
Group2=[cad]
    Capture0=[cad] Index=28 Length=3
```

Input/Output

The BCL provides a streams-based I/O framework that can handle a wide range of stream and backing store types. This support for streams also infuses the rest of the BCL, with the pattern repeating in non-I/O areas such as cryptography, HTTP support, and more.

This section describes the core stream types and provides examples. The types mentioned in this section all exist in the `System.I/O` namespace.

Streams and Backing Stores

A *stream* represents the flow of data coming in and out of a backing store. A *backing store* represents the endpoint of a stream. Although a backing store is often a file or network connection, in reality it can represent any medium capable of reading or writing raw data.

A simple example would be to use a stream to read and write to a file on disk. However, streams and backing stores are not limited to disk and network I/O. A more sophisticated example would be to use the cryptography support in the BCL to encrypt or decrypt a stream of bytes as they move around in memory.

Abstract Stream class

`Stream` is an abstract class that defines operations for reading and writing a stream of raw typeless data as bytes. Once a stream has been opened, it stays open and can be read from or written to until the stream is flushed and closed. Flushing a stream updates the writes made to the stream; closing a stream first flushes the stream, then closes the stream.

`Stream` has the methods `CanRead`, `CanWrite`, and `CanSeek`, for streams that support only sequential access. If a stream supports random access, the `SetPosition` method can move to a linear position on that stream.

The `Stream` class provides synchronous and asynchronous read and write operations. By default, an asynchronous method calls the stream's corresponding synchronous method by wrapping the synchronous method in a delegate type and starting a new thread. Similarly, by default, a synchronous method calls the stream's corresponding asynchronous method and waits until the thread has completed its operation. Classes that derive from `Stream` must override either the synchronous or asynchronous methods but may override both sets of methods if the need arises.

Concrete Stream-derived classes

The BCL includes a number of different concrete implementations of the abstract base class `Stream`. Each implementation represents a different storage medium and allows a raw stream of bytes to be read from and written to the backing store.

Examples of this include the `FileStream` class (which reads and writes bytes to and from a file) and the `NetworkStream` class (which sends and receives bytes over the network).

In addition, a stream may act as the frontend to another stream, performing additional processing on the underlying stream as needed. Examples of this include stream encryption/decryption and stream buffering.

Here is an example that creates a text file on disk and uses the abstract
File type to write data to it:

```
using System.IO;
class Test {
  static void Main() {
    Stream s = new FileStream("foo.txt", Filemode.Create);
    s.WriteByte("67");
    s.WriteByte("35");
    s.Close();
  }
}
```

Encapsulating raw streams

The Stream class defines operations for reading and writing raw typeless
data, in the form of bytes. Typically, however, you need to work with a
stream of characters, not a stream of bytes. To solve this problem, the BCL
provides the abstract base classes TextReader and TextWriter, which
define a contract to read and write a stream of characters, as well as a set
of concrete implementations.

Abstract TextReader/TextWriter classes

TextReader and TextWriter are abstract base classes that define operations for reading and writing a stream of characters. The most fundamental
operations of the TextReader and TextWriter classes are the methods
that read and write a single character to or from a stream.

The TextReader class provides default implementations for methods that
read in an array of characters or a string representing a line of characters.
The TextWriter class provides default implementations for methods that
write an array of characters, as well as methods that convert common
types (optionally with formatting options) to a sequence of characters.

The BCL includes a number of different concrete implementations of the
abstract base classes TextReader and TextWriter. Some of the most
prominent include StreamReader and StreamWriter, and String-
Reader and StringWriter.

StreamReader and StreamWriter classes

StreamReader and StreamWriter are concrete classes that derive from
TextReader and TextWriter, respectively, and operate on a Stream
(passed as a constructor parameter).

These classes allow you to combine a Stream (which can have a backing
store but only knows about raw data) with a TextReader/TextWriter
(which knows about character data, but doesn't have a backing store).

In addition, `StreamReader` and `StreamWriter` can perform special translations between characters and raw bytes. Such translations include
translating Unicode characters to ANSI characters to either big- or little-
endian format.

Here is an example that uses a `StreamWriter` wrapped around a
`FileStream` class to write to a file:

```
using System.Text;
using System.IO;
class Test {
  static void Main() {
    Stream fs = new FileStream ("foo.txt", FileMode.Create);
    StreamWriter sw = new StreamWriter(fs, Encoding.ASCII);
    sw.Write("Hello!");
    sw.Close();
  }
}
```

StringReader and StringWriter classes

`StringReader` and `StringWriter` are concrete classes that derive from
`TextReader` and `TextWriter`, respectively, and operate on a string
(passed as a constructor parameter).

The `StringReader` class can be thought of as the simplest possible read-
only backing store, because it simply performs read operations on that
string. The `StringWriter` class can be thought of as the simplest possible
write-only backing store, because it simply performs write operations on
that `StringBuilder`.

Here is an example that uses a `StringWriter` wrapped around an underlying `StringBuilder` backing store to write to a string:

```
using System;
using System.IO;
using System.Text;
class Test {
  static void Main() {
    StringBuilder sb = new StringBuilder();
    StringWriter sw = new StringWriter(sb);
    WriteHello(sw);
    Console.WriteLine(sb);
  }
  static void WriteHello(TextWriter tw) {
    tw.Write("Hello, String I/O!");
  }
}
```

Directories and Files

The `File` and `Directory` classes encapsulate the operations typically associated with file I/O, such as copying, moving, deleting, renaming, and enumerating files and directories.

The actual manipulation of the contents of a file is done with a `FileStream`. The `File` class has methods that return a `FileStream`, though you may directly instantiate a `FileStream`.

In this example, you read in and print out the contents of a text file specified on the command line:

```
using System;
using System.IO;
class Test {
    static void Main(string[] args) {
        Stream s = File.OpenRead(args[0]);
        StreamReader sr = new StreamReader(s);
        Console.WriteLine(sr.ReadLine());
        sr.Close();
    }
}
```

Networking

The BCL includes a number of types that make accessing networked resources easy. Offering different levels of abstraction, these types allow an application to ignore much of the detail normally required to access networked resources, while retaining a high degree of control.

This section describes the core networking support in the BCL, and provides numerous examples leveraging the predefined classes. The types mentioned in this section all exist in the `System.Net.Regular-Expressions` and `System.Net.Sockets` namespaces.

Network Programming Models

High-level access is performed using a set of types that implement a generic request/response architecture that is extensible to support new protocols. The implementation of this architecture in the BCL also includes HTTP-specific extensions to make interacting with web servers easy.

Should the application require lower-level access to the network, types exist to support the Transmission Control Protocol (TCP) and User Datagram Protocol (UDP). Finally, in situations where direct transport-level access is required, there are types that provide raw socket access.

Generic Request/Response Architecture

The request/response architecture is based on Uniform Resource Indicator (URI) and stream I/O, follows the factory design pattern, and makes good use of abstract types and interfaces.

A factory type (`WebRequestFactory`) parses the URI and creates the appropriate protocol handler to fulfill the request.

Protocol handlers share a common abstract base type (`WebRequest`), which exposes properties that configure the request and methods used to retrieve the response.

Responses are also represented as types and share a common abstract base type (`WebRequest`) which exposes a `NetworkStream`, providing simple streams-based I/O and easy integration into the rest of the BCL.

This example is a simple implementation of the popular Unix *snarf* utility. It demonstrates the use of the `WebRequest` and `WebResponse` classes to retrieve the contents of a URI and print them to the console:

```
// Snarf.cs - compile with /r:System.Net.dll
// Run Snarf.exe <http-uri> to retrieve a web page
using System;
using System.IO;
using System.Net;
using System.Text;
class Snarf {
  static void Main(string[] args) {

    // Retrieve the data at the URL with an WebRequest ABC
    WebRequest req = WebRequestFactory.Create(args[0]);
    WebResponse resp = req.GetResponse();

    // Read in the data, performing ASCII->Unicode encoding
    Stream s = resp.GetResponseStream();
    StreamReader sr = new StreamReader(s, Encoding.ASCII);
    string doc = sr.ReadToEnd();

    Console.WriteLine(doc); // Print result to console
  }
}
```

HTTP-Specific Support

The request/response architecture inherently supports protocol-specific extensions via the use of subtyping.

Since the `WebRequestFactory` creates and returns the appropriate handler type based on the URI, accessing protocol-specific features is as easy as downcasting the returned `WebRequest` object to the appropriate protocol-specific handler and accessing the extended functionality.

The BCL includes specific support for the HTTP protocol, including the ability to easily access and control elements of an interactive web session, such as the HTTP headers, user-agent strings, proxy support, user credentials, authentication, keep-alives, pipelining, and more.

This example demonstrates the use of the HTTP-specific request/response classes to control the user-agent string for the request and retrieve the server type:

```
// ProbeSvr.cs - compile with /r:System.Net.dll
// Run ProbeSvr.exe <servername> to retrieve the server type
using System;
using System.Net;
class ProbeSvr {
  static void Main(string[] args) {

    // Get instance of WebRequest ABC, convert to HttpWebRequest
    WebRequest req = WebRequestFactory.Create(args[0]);
    HttpWebRequest httpReq = (HttpWebRequest)req;

    // Access HTTP-specific features such as User-Agent
    httpReq.UserAgent = "CSPRProbe/1.0";

    // Retrieve response and print to console
    WebResponse resp = req.GetResponse();
    HttpWebResponse httpResp = (HttpWebResponse)resp;
    Console.WriteLine(httpResp.Server);
  }
}
```

Adding New Protocol Handlers

Adding handlers to support new protocols is trivial: simply implement a new set of derived types based on `WebRequest` and `WebResponse`, implement the `IWebRequestCreate` interface on your `WebRequest`-derived type, and register it as a new protocol handler with the `WebRequestFactory` at runtime. Once this is done, any code that uses the request/response architecture can access networked resources using the new URI format (and underlying protocol).

Using TCP, UDP, and Sockets

The `System.Net.Sockets` namespace includes types that provide protocol-level support for TCP and UDP. These types are built on the underlying `Socket` type, which is itself directly accessible for transport-level access to the network.

Two classes provide the TCP support: **TCPListener** and **TCPClient**. **TCPListener** listens for incoming connections, creating **Socket** instances that respond to the connection request. **TCPClient** connects to a remote host, hiding the details of the underlying socket in a **Stream**-derived type that allows stream I/O over the network.

A class called **UDPClient** provides the UDP support. **UDPClient** serves as both a client and a listener and includes multicast support, allowing individual datagrams to be sent and received as byte arrays.

Both the TCP and the UDP classes help to access the underlying network socket (represented by the **Socket** class). The **Socket** class is a thin wrapper over the native Windows sockets functionality and is the lowest level of networking accessible to managed code.

The following example is a simple implementation of the Quote of the Day (QUOTD) protocol, as defined by the IETF in RFC 865. It demonstrates the use of a TCP listener to accept incoming requests and the use of the lower-level **Socket** type to fulfill the request:

```csharp
// QOTDListener.cs - compile with /r:System.Net.dll
// Run QOTDListener.exe to service incoming QOTD requests
using System;
using System.Net;
using System.Net.Sockets;
using System.Text;
class QOTDListener {
   static string[] quotes =
{@"Sufficiently advanced magic is indistinguishable from technology --
Terry Pratchett",
 @"Sufficiently advanced technology is indistinguishable from magic --
 Arthur C Clarke" };
   static void Main() {

     // Start a TCP listener on port 17
     TCPListener l = new TCPListener(17);
     l.Start();
     Console.WriteLine("Waiting for clients to connect");
     Console.WriteLine("Press Ctrl+C to quit...");
     int numServed = 1;
     while (true) {

       // Block waiting for an incoming socket connect request
       Socket s = l.Accept();

       // Encode alternating quotes as bytes for sending
       Char[] carr = quotes[numServed%2].ToCharArray();
       Byte[] barr = Encoding.ASCII.GetBytes(carr);

       // Return data to client, then clean up socket & repeat
       s.Send(barr, barr.Length, 0);
       s.Shutdown(SocketShutdown.SdBoth);
```

```
      s.Close();
      Console.WriteLine("{0} quotes served...", numServed++);
    }
  }
}
```

To test this example, run the listener and try connecting to port 17 on *localhost* using a *telnet* client. (Under Windows 2000, this can be done from the command line by entering: `telnet localhost 17`).

Notice the use of `Socket.Shutdown` and `Socket.Close` at the end of the `while` loop; this is required to flush and close the socket immediately, rather than wait for the garbage collector to finalize and collect unreachable `Socket` objects later.

Using DNS

The networking types in the base class library also support normal and reverse Domain Name System (DNS) resolution. Here's an example using these types:

```
// DNSLookup.cs - compile with /r:System.Net.dll
// Run DNSLookup.exe <servername> to determine IP addresses
using System;
using System.Net;
class DNSLookup {
  static void Main(string[] args) {
    IPHostEntry he = DNS.GetHostByName(args[0]);
    IPAddress[] addrs = he.AddressList;
    foreach (IPAddress addr in addrs)
      Console.WriteLine(addr);
  }
}
```

Threading

A C# application runs in one or more *threads* that effectively execute in parallel within the same application. Here is a simple multithreaded application:

```
using System;
using System.Threading;
class ThreadTest {
  static void Main() {
  Thread t = new Thread(new ThreadStart(Go));
    t.Start();
    Go();
  }
  static void Go() {
    for (char c='a'; c<='z'; c++ )
```

```
        Console.Write(c);
    }
  }
```

In this example, a new thread object is constructed by passing it a
ThreadStart delegate that wraps the method that specifies where to start
execution for that thread. You then start the thread and call Go, so two
separate threads are running Go in parallel. However, there's a problem:
both threads share a common resource—the console. If you run **Thread-
Test**, you get output something like this:

    abcdabcdefghijklmnopqrsefghjiklmnopqrstuvwxyztuvwxyz

Thread Synchronization

Thread synchronization comprises techniques for ensuring that multiple
threads coordinate their access to shared resources.

The lock statement

C# provides the **lock** statement to ensure that only one thread at a time
can access a block of code. Consider the following example:

```
using System;
using System.Threading;
class LockTest {
  static void Main() {
    LockTest lt = new LockTest ();
    Thread t = new Thread(new ThreadStart(lt.Go));
    t.Start();
    lt.Go();
  }
  void Go() {
    lock(this)
      for ( char c='a'; c<='z'; c++)
        Console.Write(c);
  }
}
```

Running **LockTest** produces the following output:

    abcdefghijklmnopqrstuvwzyzabcdefghijklmnopqrstuvwzyz

The **lock** statement acquires a lock on any reference type instance. If
another thread has already acquired the lock, the thread doesn't continue
until the other thread relinquishes its lock on that instance.

The **lock** statement is actually a syntactic shortcut for calling the **Enter**
and **Exit** methods of the BCL **Monitor** class (see the upcoming section
"Monitor Class"):

```
System.Threading.Monitor.Enter(expression);
try {
```

```
    ...
}
finally {
  System.Threading.Monitor.Exit(expression);
}
```

Pulse and Wait operations

In combination with locks, the next most common threading operations
are `Pulse` and `Wait`. These operations let threads communicate with each
other via a monitor that maintains a list of threads waiting to grab an
object's lock:

```
using System;
using System.Threading;
class MonitorTest {
  static void Main() {
    MonitorTest mt = new MonitorTest();
    Thread t = new Thread(new ThreadStart(mt.Go));
    t.Start();
    mt.Go();
  }
  void Go() {
    for ( char c='a'; c<='z'; c++)
      lock(this) {
        Console.Write(c);
        Monitor.Pulse(this);
        Monitor.Wait(this);
      }
  }
}
```

Running `MonitorTest` produces the following result:

aabbccddeeffgghhiijjkkllmmnnooppqqrrssttuuvvwwxxyyzz

The `Pulse` method tells the monitor to wake up the next thread that is
waiting to get a lock on that object as soon as the current thread has
released it. The current thread typically releases the monitor in one of two
ways. First, execution may leave the `lock` statement blocked. The second
way is to call the `Wait` method, which temporarily releases the lock on an
object and makes the thread fall asleep until another thread wakes it up
by pulsing the object.

Deadlocks

The `MonitorTest` example actually contains a type of bug called a *deadlock*. When you run the program, it prints the correct output, but then the
console window locks up. This is because there are two sleeping threads,
and neither will wake the other. The deadlock occurs because when

printing z, each thread goes to sleep but never gets pulsed. You can solve
the problem by replacing the Go method with this new implementation:

```
void Go() {
  for ( char c='a'; c<='z'; c++)
    lock(this) {
      Console.Write(c);
      Monitor.Pulse(this);
      if (c<'z')
        Monitor.Wait(this);
    }
}
```

In general, the danger of using locks is that two threads may both end up
being blocked waiting for a resource held by the other thread. Most
common deadlock situations can be avoided by ensuring that you always
acquire resources in the same order.

Atomic operations

Atomic operations are operations the system promises will not be interrupted. In the previous examples, the method Go isn't atomic, because it
can be interrupted while it is running so another thread can run.
However, updating a variable is atomic, because the operation is guaranteed to complete without control being passed to another thread. The
Interlocked class provides additional atomic operations, which allows
basic operations to be performed without requiring a lock. This can be
useful, since acquiring a lock is many times slower than a simple atomic
operation.

Common Thread Types

Much of the functionality of threads is provided through the classes in the
System.Threading namespace. The most basic thread class to understand is the Monitor class, which is explained in the following section.

Monitor Class

The System.Threading.Monitor class provides an implementation of
Hoare's Monitor that allows you to use any reference-type instance as a
monitor.

Enter and Exit methods

The Enter and Exit methods, respectively, obtain and release a lock on
an object. If the object is already held by another thread, Enter waits
until the lock is released, or the thread is interrupted by a Thread-
InterruptedException. Every call to Enter for a given object on a

thread should be matched with a call to Exit for the same object on the same thread.

TryEnter methods

The TryEnter methods are similar to the Enter method, but they don't require a lock on the object to proceed. These methods return true if the lock is obtained, and false if it isn't, optionally passing in a timeout parameter that specifies the maximum time to wait for the other threads to relinquish the lock.

Wait methods

The thread holding a lock on an object may call one of the Wait methods to temporarily release the lock and block itself, while it waits for another thread to notify it by executing a pulse on the monitor. This approach can tell a worker thread that there is work to perform on that object. The overloaded versions of Wait allow you to specify a timeout that reactivates the thread if a pulse hasn't arrived within the specified duration. When the thread wakes up, it reacquires the monitor for the object (potentially blocking until the monitor becomes available). Wait returns true if the thread is reactivated by another thread pulsing the monitor and returns false if the Wait call times out without receiving a pulse.

Pulse and PulseAll methods

A thread holding a lock on an object may call Pulse on that object to wake up a blocked thread as soon as the thread calling Pulse has released its lock on the monitor. If multiple threads are waiting on the same monitor, Pulse activates only the first in the queue (successive calls to Pulse wake up other waiting threads, one per call). The PulseAll method successively wakes up all the threads.

Assemblies

An *assembly* is a logical package (similar to a DLL in Win32) that consists of a manifest, a set of one or more modules, and an optional set of resources. This package forms the basic unit of deployment and versioning, and creates a boundary for type resolution and security permissioning.

Elements of an Assembly

Every .NET application consists of at least one assembly, which is in turn built from a number of basic elements.

The *manifest* contains a set of metadata that describes everything the runtime needs to know about the assembly. This information includes:

- The textual name of the assembly

- The version number of the assembly

- An optional shared name and signed assembly hash

- The list of files in the assembly with file hashes

- The list of referenced assemblies, including versioning information and an optional public key

- The list of types included in the assembly, with a mapping to the module containing the type

- The set of minimum and optional security permissions requested by the assembly

- The set of security permissions explicitly refused by the assembly

- Culture, processor, and OS information

- A set of custom attributes to capture details such as product name, owner information, etc.

Modules contain types described using metadata and implemented using MSIL.

Resources contain nonexecutable data that is logically included with the assembly. Examples of this include bitmaps, localizable text, persisted objects, etc.

Packaging

The simplest assembly contains a manifest and a single module containing the application's types, packaged as an EXE with a `Main` entry point. More complex assemblies can include multiple modules (Portable Executable (PE) files), separate resource files, manifest, etc.

The manifest is generally included in one of the existing PE files in the assembly, although the manifest can also be a standalone PE file.

Modules are PE files, typically DLLs or EXEs. Only one module in an assembly can contain an entry point (either `Main`, `WinMain`, or `DllMain`).

An assembly may also contain multiple modules. This technique can reduce the working set of the application, as the CLR loads only the required modules. In addition, each module can be written in a different language, allowing a mixture of C#, VB.NET, and raw MSIL. Although not common, a single module could also be included in several different assemblies.

Finally, an assembly may contain a set of resources, which can either be kept in standalone files or included in one of the PE files in the assembly.

Deployment

An assembly is the smallest .NET unit of deployment. Due to the self-describing nature of a manifest, deployment can be as simple as copying the assembly (and in the case of a multifile assembly, all the associated files) into a directory.

This is a vast improvement over traditional COM development where components, their supporting DLLs, and their configuration information are spread out over multiple directories and the Windows registry.

Generally, assemblies are deployed into the application directory and are not shared. These are called *private assemblies*. However, assemblies can also be shared between applications, and these are called *shared assemblies*. To share an assembly you need to give it a *shared name* (also known as a "strong" name) and deploy it in the global assembly cache.

The shared name consists of a name, a public key, and a digital signature. The shared name is included in the assembly manifest and forms the unique identifier for the assembly.

The global assembly cache is a machine-wide storage area that contains assemblies intended for use by multiple applications.

For more information on working with shared assemblies and the global assembly cache, see "Sharing Assemblies" in Appendix E, *Working with Assemblies*.

Versioning

The manifest of an application contains a version number for the assembly and a list of all the referenced assemblies with associated version information. Assembly version numbers are divided into four parts and look like this:

```
<major>.<minor>.<build>.<revision>
```

This information is used to mitigate versioning problems as assemblies evolve over time.

At runtime, the CLR uses the version information specified in the manifest and a set of versioning policies defined for the machine to determine which versions of each dependent, shared assembly to load.

The default versioning policy for shared assemblies automatically uses the newest available version with matching major and minor version numbers. By changing a configuration file, the application or an administrator can override this behavior.

Private assemblies have no versioning policy, and the CLR simply loads the newest assemblies found in the application directory.

Type Resolution

The unique identifier for a type (known as a **TypeRef**) consists of a reference to the assembly it was defined in and the fully qualified type name (including any namespaces). For example, this local variable declaration:

```
System.Net.WebRequest wr;
```

is represented in MSIL assembly language as follows:

```
.assembly extern System.Net { .ver 1:0:2204:4 ... }
.locals(class [System.Net]System.Net.WebRequest wr)
```

In this example, the **System.Net.WebRequest** type is scoped to the **System.Net** shared assembly, which is identified using a shared name and associated version number.

When your application starts, the CLR attempts to resolve all static TypeRefs by locating the correct versions of each dependent assembly (as determined by the versioning policy) and verifying that the types actually exist (ignoring any access modifiers).

When your application attempts to use the type, the CLR verifies that you have the correct level of access and throws runtime exceptions if there is a versioning incompatibility.

Security Permissions

The assembly forms a boundary for security permissioning.

The assembly manifest contains hashes for any referenced assemblies (determined at compile time), a list of the minimum set of security permissions the assembly *requires* in order to function, a list of the optional permissions that it *requests*, and a list of the permissions that it explicitly *refuses* (i.e., never wants to receive).

To illustrate how these permissions might be used, imagine an email client similar to Microsoft Outlook, developed using the .NET Framework. It probably requires the ability to communicate over the network on ports 110 (POP3), 25 (SMTP), and 143 (IMAP4). It might request the ability to run Javascript functions in a sandbox to allow full interactivity when presenting HTML emails. Finally, it probably refuses ever being granted the ability to write to disk or read the local address book, thus avoiding scripting attacks such as the *ILoveYou* virus.

Essentially, the assembly declares its security needs and assumptions, but leaves the final decision on permissioning up to the CLR, which enforces local security policy.

At runtime the CLR uses the hashes to determine if a dependent assembly has been tampered with and combines the assembly permission information with local security policy to determine whether to load the assembly and which permissions to grant it.

This mechanism provides fine-grained control over security and is a major advantage of the .NET Framework over traditional Windows applications.

Reflection

Many of the services available in .NET and exposed via C# (such as late binding, serialization, remoting, attributes, etc.) depend on the presence of metadatas. Your own programs can also take advantage of this metadata, and even extend it with new information.

Manipulating existing types via their metadata is termed *reflection* and is done using a rich set of types in the `System.Reflection` namespace. Creating new types (and associated metadata) is termed `Reflection.Emit`, and is done via the types in the `System.Reflection.Emit` namespace. You can extend the metadata for existing types with custom attributes. For more information, see the later section "Custom Attributes."

Type Hierarchy

Reflection involves traversing and manipulating an object model that represents an application, including all its compile-time and runtime elements. Consequently, it is important to understand the various logical units of a .NET application and their roles and relationships.

The fundamental units of an application are its types, which contain members and nested types. In addition to types, an application contains one or more modules and one or more assemblies. All these elements are static and are described in metadata produced by the compiler at compile time. The one exception to this rule are elements (such as types, modules, assemblies, etc.) that are created on the fly via `Reflection.Emit`, which is described in the later section "Creating New Types at Runtime."

At runtime, these elements are all contained within an `AppDomain`. An `AppDomain` isn't described with metadata, yet it plays an important role in reflection because it forms the root of the type hierarchy of a .NET application at runtime.

In any given application, the relationship between these units is hierarchical, as depicted by the diagram below:

```
AppDomain (runtime root of hierarchy)
   Assemblies
      Modules
         Types
            Members
            Nested types
```

Each of these elements is discussed in the following sections.

Types, members, and nested types

The most basic element that reflection deals with is the type. This class represents the metadata for each type declaration in an application (both predefined and user-defined types).

Types contain members, which include constructors, fields, properties, events, and methods. In addition, types may contain nested types, which exist within the scope of an outer type and are typically used as helper classes. Types are grouped into modules, which are, in turn, contained within assemblies.

Assemblies and modules

Assemblies are the logical equivalent of DLLs in Win32 and the basic unit of deployment, versioning, and reuse for types. In addition, assemblies create a security, visibility, and scope resolution boundary for types (see the earlier section "Assemblies").

A module is a physical file such as a DLL, an EXE, or a resource (such as GIFs or JPGs). While it isn't common practice, an assembly can be composed of multiple modules, allowing you to control application working set size, use multiple languages within one assembly, and share a module across multiple assemblies.

AppDomains

From the perspective of reflection, an AppDomain is the root of the type hierarchy and serves as the container for assemblies and types when they are loaded into memory at runtime. A helpful way to think about an AppDomain is to view it as the logical equivalent of a process in a Win32 application.

AppDomains provide isolation, creating a hard boundary for managed code just like the process boundary under Win32. Similar to processes, AppDomains can be started and stopped independently, and application faults take down only the AppDomain the fault occurs in, not the process hosting the AppDomain.

Retrieving the Type for an Instance

At the heart of reflection is System.Type, which is an abstract base class that provides access to the metadata of a type.

You can access the Type class for any instance using GetType, which is a nonvirtual method of System.Object. When you call GetType, the method returns a concrete subtype of System.Type, which can reflect over and manipulate the type.

Retrieving a Type Directly

You can also retrieve a Type class by name (without needing an instance) using the static method GetType on the Type class, as follows:

```
Type t = Type.GetType("System.Int32");
```

Finally, C# provides the typeof operator, which returns the Type class for any type known at compile time:

```
Type t = typeof(System.Int32);
```

The main difference between these two approaches is that Type.GetType is evaluated at runtime and is more dynamic, binding by name; while the typeof operator is evaluated at compile time, uses a type token, and is slightly faster to call.

Reflecting over a Type Hierarchy

Once you have retrieved a Type instance you can navigate the application hierarchy described earlier, accessing the metadata via types that represent members, modules, assemblies, namespaces, AppDomains, and nested types. You can also inspect the metadata and any custom attributes, create new instances of the types, and invoke members.

Here is an example that uses reflection to display the members in three different types:

```
using System;
using System.Reflection;
class Test {
  static void Main() {
    object o = new Object();
    DumpTypeInfo(o.GetType());
    DumpTypeInfo(typeof(int));
    DumpTypeInfo(Type.GetType("System.String"));
  }
  static void DumpTypeInfo(Type t) {
    Console.WriteLine("Type: {0}", t);

    // Retrieve the list of members in the type
    MemberInfo[] miarr = t.GetMembers(BindingFlags.LookupAll);

    // Print out details on each of them
    foreach (MemberInfo mi in miarr)
      Console.WriteLine("  {0}={1}", mi.MemberType.Format(), mi);
  }
}
```

Late Binding to Types

Reflection can also perform *late binding*, in which the application dynamically loads, instantiates, and uses a type at runtime. This provides greater flexibility at the expense of invocation overhead.

In this section, we create an example that uses very late binding, dynamically discovers new types at runtime, and uses them.

In the example one or more assemblies are loaded by name (as specified on the command line) and iterated through the types in the assembly looking for subtypes of the **Greeting** abstract base class. When one is found, the type is instantiated and its **SayHello** method invoked, which displays an appropriate greeting.

To perform the runtime discovery of types, we use an abstract base class that's compiled into an assembly as follows (see the source comment for filename and compilation information):

```
// Greeting.cs - compile with /t:library
public abstract class Greeting {
  public abstract void SayHello();
}
```

Compiling this code produces a file named *Greeting.dll*, which the other parts of the sample can use.

We now create a new assembly containing two concrete subtypes of the abstract type `Greeting`, as follows (see the source comment for filename and compilation information):

```csharp
// English.cs - compile with /t:library /r:Greeting.dll
using System;
public class AmericanGreeting : Greeting {
  private string msg = "Hey, dude. Wassup!";
  public override void SayHello() {
    Console.WriteLine(msg);
  }
}
public class BritishGreeting : Greeting {
  private string msg = "Good morning, old chap!";
  public override void SayHello() {
    Console.WriteLine(msg);
  }
}
```

Compiling the source file *English.cs* produces a file named *English.dll*, which the main program can now dynamically reflect over and use.

Now we create the main sample, as follows (see the source comment for filename and compilation information):

```csharp
// SayHello.cs - compile with /r:Greeting.dll
// Run with SayHello.exe <dllname1> <dllname2> ... <dllnameN>
using System;
using System.Reflection;
class Test {
  static void Main (string[] args) {

    // Iterate over the cmd-line options,
    // trying to load each assembly
    foreach (string s in args) {
      Assembly a = Assembly.LoadFrom(s);

      // Pick through all the public type, looking for
      // subtypes of the abstract base class Greeting
      foreach (Type t in a.GetTypes())
        if (t.IsSubclassOf(typeof(Greeting))) {

          // Having found an appropriate subtype, create it
          object o = Activator.CreateInstance(t);

          // Retrieve the SayHello MethodInfo & invoke it
          MethodInfo mi = t.GetMethod("SayHello");
          mi.Invoke(o, null);
        }
```

```
       }
     }
   }
```

Running the sample now with *SayHello English.dll* produces the following output:

```
Hey, dude. Wassup!
Good morning, old chap!
```

The interesting aspect of the preceding sample is that it's completely late-bound; i.e., long after the *SayHello* program is shipped you can create a new type and have *SayHello* automatically take advantage of it by simply specifying it on the command line. This is one of the key benefits of late binding via reflection.

Activation

In the previous examples, we loaded an assembly by hand and used the **System.Activator** class to create a new instance based on a type. There are many overrides of the **CreateInstance** method that provide a wide range of creation options, including the ability to short-circuit the process and create a type directly:

```
object o = Activator.CreateInstance("Assem1.dll",
                         "Friendly.Greeting");
```

Other capabilities of the **Activator** type include creating types on remote machines, creating types in specific **AppDomains** (sandboxes), and creating types by invoking a specific constructor (rather than using the default constructor as these examples show).

Advanced Uses of Reflection

The preceding example demonstrates the use of reflection, but doesn't perform any tasks you can't accomplish using normal C# language constructs. However, reflection can also manipulate types in ways not supported directly in C#, as is demonstrated in this section.

While the CLR enforces access controls on type members (specified using access modifiers such as **private** and **protected**), these restrictions don't apply to reflection. Assuming you have the correct set of permissions, you can use reflection to access and manipulate private data and function members, as this example using the **Greeting** subtypes from the previous section shows (see the source comment for filename and compilation information):

```
// InControl.cs - compile with /r:Greeting.dll,English.dll
using System;
```

```
using System.Reflection;
class TestReflection {
  // Note: This method requires the ReflectionPermission perm.
  static void ModifyPrivateData(object o, string msg) {

    // Get a FieldInfo type for the private data member
    Type t = o.GetType();
    FieldInfo fi = t.GetField("msg", BindingFlags.NonPublic|
                                     BindingFlags.Instance);

    // Use the FieldInfo to adjust the data member value
    fi.SetValue(o, msg);
  }
  static void Main() {
    // Create instances of both types
    BritishGreeting bg = new BritishGreeting();
    AmericanGreeting ag = new AmericanGreeting();

    // Adjust the private data via reflection
    ModifyPrivateData(ag, "Things are not the way they seem");
    ModifyPrivateData(bg, "The runtime is in total control!");

    // Display the modified greeting strings
    ag.SayHello(); // "Things are not the way they seem"
    bg.SayHello(); // "The runtime is in total control!"
  }
}
```

When run, this sample generates the following output:

```
Things are not the way they seem
The runtime is in total control!
```

This demonstrates that the private msg data members in both types are modified via reflection, although there are no public members defined on the types that allow that operation. Note that while this technique can bypass access controls, it still doesn't violate type safety.

Although this is a somewhat contrived example, the capability can be useful when building utilities such as class browsers and test suite automation tools that need to inspect and interact with a type at a deeper level than its public interface.

Creating New Types at Runtime

The System.Reflection.Emit namespace contains classes that can create entirely new types at runtime. These classes can define a dynamic assembly in memory; define a dynamic module in the assembly; define a new type in the module, including all its members; and emit the MSIL opcodes needed to implement the application logic in the members.

Here is an example that creates and uses a new type called `HelloWorld` with a member called `SayHello`:

```
using System;
using System.Reflection;
using System.Reflection.Emit;
public class Test
{
  static void Main()
  {
    // Create a dynamic assembly in the current AppDomain
    AppDomain ad = AppDomain.CurrentDomain;
    AssemblyName an = new AssemblyName();
    an.Name = "DynAssembly";
    AssemblyBuilder ab =
      ad.DefineDynamicAssembly(an, AssemblyBuilderAccess.Run);

    // Create a module in the assembly & a type in the module
    Assembly a = (Assembly)ab;
    ModuleBuilder modb = a.DefineDynamicModule("DynModule");
    TypeBuilder tb = modb.DefineType("AgentSmith",
                                     TypeAttributes.Public);

    // Add a SayHello member to the type
    MethodBuilder mb = tb.DefineMethod("SayHello",
                                       MethodAttributes.Public,
                                       null, null);

    // Generate the MSIL for the SayHello Member
    ILGenerator ilg = mb.GetILGenerator();
    ilg.EmitWriteLine("Never send a human to do a machine's job.");
    ilg.Emit(OpCodes.Ret);

    // Finalize the type so we can create it
    tb.CreateType();

    // Create an instance of the new type
    Type t = Type.GetType("AgentSmith");
    object o = Activator.CreateInstance(t);

    // Prints "Never send a human to do a machine's job."
    t.GetMethod("SayHello").Invoke(o, null);
  }
}
```

A common example using `Reflection.Emit` is the regular-expression support in the BCL, which can emit new types that are tuned to search for specific regular expressions, eliminating the overhead of interpreting the regular expression at runtime.

Other uses of `Reflection.Emit` in the BCL include dynamically generating transparent proxies for remoting and generating types that perform specific XSLT transforms with the minimum runtime overhead.

Custom Attributes

Types, members, modules, and assemblies all have associated metadata that is used by all the major CLR services, is considered an indivisible part of an application, and can be accessed via reflection (see the earlier section "Reflection").

A key characteristic of metadata is that it can be extended. You extend the metadata with *custom attributes*, which allow you to "decorate" a code element with additional information stored in the metadata associated with the element.

This additional information can then be retrieved at runtime and used to build services that work *declaratively*, which is the way that the CLR implements core features such as serialization and interception.

Language Support for Custom Attributes

Decorating an element with a custom attribute is known as *specifying* the custom attribute and is done by writing the name of the attribute enclosed in brackets ([]) immediately before the element declaration as follows:

```
[Serializable] public class Foo {...}
```

In this example, the `Foo` class is specified as serializable. This information is saved in the metadata for `Foo`, and affects the way the CLR treats an instance of this class.

A useful way to think about custom attributes is that they expand the built-in set of declarative constructs in the C# language such as `public`, `private`, and `sealed`.

Compiler Support for Custom Attributes

In reality, custom attributes are simply types derived from `System.Attribute` with language constructs for specifying them on an element (see the section "Attributes" in Chapter 2).

These language constructs are recognized by the compiler, which emits a small chunk of data into the metadata. This custom data includes a serialized call to the constructor of the custom attribute type (containing the values for the positional parameters), and a collection of property set operations (containing the values for the named parameters).

The compiler also recognizes a small number of *pseudo-custom attributes*. These are special attributes that have direct representation in metadata and are stored natively (i.e., not as chunks of custom data). This is primarily a runtime performance optimization, although it has some implications for retrieving attributes via reflection, as discussed later.

To understand this, consider the following class with two specified attributes:

```
[Serializable, Obsolete]
class Foo {...}
```

When compiled, the metadata for the class Foo looks like this in MSIL:

```
.class private auto ansi serializable Foo {
  .custom instance void
    System.ObsoleteAttribute::.ctor() = ( 01 00 00 00 )
    ...
  }
}
```

Compare the different treatment by the compiler of the Obsolete attribute, which is a custom attribute and is stored as a serialized constructor call to the System.ObsoleteAttribute type, to the treatment of the Serializable attribute, which is a pseudo-custom attribute represented directly in the metadata with the serializable token.

Runtime Support for Custom Attributes

At runtime the core CLR services such as serialization and remoting inspect the custom and pseudo-custom attributes to determine how to handle an instance of a type.

In the case of custom attributes, this is done by creating an instance of the attribute (invoking the relevant constructor call and property-set operations), and then performing whatever steps are needed to determine how to handle an instance of the type.

In the case of pseudo-custom attributes, this is done by simply inspecting the metadata directly and determining how to handle an instance of the type. Consequently, handling pseudo-custom attributes is more efficient than handling custom attributes.

Note that none of these steps is initiated until a service or user program actually tries to access the attributes, so there is little runtime overhead unless required.

Predefined Attributes

The .NET Framework makes extensive use of attributes for purposes ranging from simple documentation to advanced support for threading, remoting, serialization, and COM interop. These attributes are all defined in the BCL, and can be used, extended, and retrieved by your own code.

However, certain attributes are treated specially by the compiler and the runtime. Three attributes considered general enough to be defined in the C# specification are AttributeUsage, Conditional, and Obsolete. Other attributes such as CLSCompliant, Serializable, and NonSerialized are also treated specially.

AttributeUsage attribute

```
[AttributeUsage(target-enum
    [, AllowMultiple=[true|false]]?
    [, Inherited=[true|false]]?
    ] (for classes)
```

The AttributeUsage attribute is applied to a new attribute class declaration. It controls how the new attribute should be treated by the compiler, specifically, what set of targets (classes, interfaces, properties, methods, parameters, etc.) the new attribute can be specified on, whether multiple instances of this attribute may be applied to the same target, and whether this attribute propagates to subtypes of the target.

target-enum is a bitwise mask of values from the System. AttributeTargets enum, which looks like this:

```
namespace System {
  [Flags]
  public enum AttributeTargets {
    Assembly      = 0x0001,
    Module        = 0x0002,
    Class         = 0x0004,
    Struct        = 0x0008,
    Enum          = 0x0010,
    Constructor   = 0x0020,
    Method        = 0x0040,
    Property      = 0x0080,
    Field         = 0x0100,
    Event         = 0x0200,
    Interface     = 0x0400,
    Parameter     = 0x0800,
    Delegate      = 0x1000,
    ReturnValue   = 0x2000,
    All           = 0x3fff,
    ClassMembers  = 0x17fc,
  }
}
```

Conditional attribute

`[Conditional`*`(symbol)`*`]` (for methods)

The `Conditional` attribute can be applied to any method with a `void` return type. The presence of this attribute tells the compiler to conditionally omit calls to the method unless *symbol* is defined in the calling code. This is similar to wrapping every call to the method with `#if` and `#endif` preprocessor directives, but `Conditional` has the advantage of needing to be specified only in one place.

Obsolete attribute

`[Obsolete([Message=]?` *message*
   `IsError=` `[true|false]]`
] (for all attribute targets)

Applied to any valid attribute target, the `Obsolete` attribute indicates that the target is obsolete. `Obsolete` can include a message that explains which alternative types or members to use and a flag that tells the compiler to treat the use of this type or member as either a warning or an error.

For example, referencing type `Bar` in the following example causes the compiler to display an error message and halts compilation:

```
[Obsolete("Don't try this at home", IsError=true)]
class Bar { ... }
```

CLSCompliant attribute

`[CLSCompliant(true|false)]`
(for all attribute targets)

Applied to an assembly, the `CLSCompliant` attribute tells the compiler whether to validate CLS compliance for all the exported types in the assembly. Applied to any other attribute target, this attribute allows the target to declare if it should be considered CLS-compliant. In order to mark a target as CLS-compliant, the entire assembly needs to be considered as such.

In the following example, the `CLSCompliant` attribute is used to specify an assembly as CLS-compliant and a class within it as not CLS-compliant:

```
[assembly:CLSCompliant(true)]

[CLSCompliant(false)]
public class Bar {
  public ushort Answer { get {return 42;} }
}
```

Serializable attribute

```
[Serializable]
```
(for classes, structs, enums, delegates)

Applied to a class, struct, enum, or delegate, the `Serializable` attribute marks it as being serializable. This attribute is a pseudo-custom attribute and is represented specially in the metadata.

NonSerialized attribute

```
[NonSerialized] (for fields)
```

Applied to a field, the `NonSerialized` attribute prevents it from being serialized along with its containing class or struct. This attribute is a pseudo-custom attribute and is represented specially in the metadata.

Defining a New Custom Attribute

In addition to using the predefined attributes supplied by the .NET Framework, you can also create your own.

To create a custom attribute:

1. Derive a class from `System.Attribute` or from a descendent of `System.Attribute`. By convention the class name should end with the word "Attribute," although this isn't required.

2. Provide the class with a public constructor. The parameters to the constructor define the positional parameters of the attribute and are mandatory when specifying the attribute on an element.

3. Declare public-instance fields, public-instance read/write properties, or public-instance write-only properties to specify the named parameters of the attribute. Unlike positional parameters, these are optional when specifying the attribute on an element.

   The types that can be used for attribute constructor parameters and properties are `bool`, `byte`, `char`, `double`, `float`, `int`, `long`, `short`, `string`, `object`, the `Type` type, `enum`, or a one-dimensional array of the aforementioned types.

4. Finally, define what the attribute, may be specified on using the `AttributeUsage` attribute, as described in the preceding section.

Consider the following example of a custom attribute, `CrossRef-Attribute`, which removes the limitation that the CLR metadata contains information about statically linked types but not dynamically linked ones.

```
using System;
[AttributeUsage(AttributeTargets.ClassMembers, AllowMultiple=true)]
class CrossRefAttribute : Attribute {
  Type   xref;
  string desc = "";
  public string Description { set { desc=value; } }
  public CrossRefAttribute(Type xref) { this.xref=xref; }
  public override string ToString() {
    string tmp = (desc.Length>0) ? " ("+desc+")" : "";
    return "CrossRef to "+xref.ToString()+tmp;
  }
}
```

From the attribute user's perspective, this attribute can be applied to any class member multiple times (note the use of the `AttributeUsage` attribute to control this). `CrossRefAttribute` takes one mandatory positional parameter (namely the type to cross reference) and one optional named parameter (the description), and is used as follows:

```
[CrossRef(typeof(Bar), Description="Foos often hang around Bars")]
class Foo {...}
```

Essentially, this attribute embeds cross references to dynamically linked types (with optional descriptions) in the metadata. This information can then be retrieved at runtime by a class browser to present a more complete view of a type's dependencies.

Retrieving a Custom Attribute at Runtime

Retrieving attributes at runtime is done using reflection via one of the `GetCustomAttribute` overloads on the object's `Type` instance. This is one of the few circumstances where the difference between custom attributes and pseudo-custom attributes becomes apparent, since pseudo-custom attributes can't be retrieved with `GetCustomAttribute`.

Here is an example that uses reflection to determine what attributes are on a specific type:

```
using System;
[Serializable, Obsolete]
class Test {
  static void Main() {
    Type t = typeof(Test);
    object[] caarr = t.GetCustomAttributes();
    Console.WriteLine("{0} has {1} custom attribute(s)",
                      t, caarr.Length);
    foreach (object ca in caarr)
      Console.WriteLine(ca);
  }
}
```

Although the `Test` class of the preceding example has two attributes specified, the sample produces the following output:

```
Test has 1 custom attribute(s)
System.ObsoleteAttribute
```

This demonstrates how the `Serializable` attribute (a pseudo-custom attribute) isn't accessible via reflection, while the `Obsolete` attribute (a custom attribute) still is.

Automatic Memory Management

Almost all modern programming languages allocate memory in two places: on the stack and on the heap.

Memory allocated on the stack stores local variables, parameters, and return values, and is generally managed automatically by the operating system.

Memory allocated on the heap, however, is treated differently by different languages. In C and C++, memory allocated on the heap is managed manually. In C# and Java, however, memory allocated on the heap is managed automatically.

While manual memory management has the advantage of being simple for runtimes to implement, it has drawbacks that tend not to exist in systems that offer automatic memory management. For example, a large percentage of bugs in C and C++ programs stem from using an object after it has been deleted (dangling pointers) or from forgetting to delete an object when it is no longer needed (memory leaks).

The process of automatically managing memory is known as *garbage collection*. While generally more complex for runtimes to implement than traditional manual memory management, garbage collection greatly simplifies development and eliminates many common errors related to manual memory management.

For example, it is almost impossible to generate a traditional memory leak in C#, and common bugs such as circular references in traditional COM development simply go away.

The Garbage Collector

C# depends on the CLR for many of its runtime services, and garbage collection is no exception.

The CLR includes a high-performing generational mark-and-compact garbage collector (GC) that performs automatic memory management for type instances stored on the managed heap.

The GC is considered to be a *tracing* garbage collector in that it doesn't interfere with every access to an object, but rather wakes up intermittently and traces the graph of objects stored on the managed heap to determine which objects can be considered garbage and therefore collected.

The GC generally initiates a garbage collection when a memory allocation occurs, and memory is too low to fulfill the request. This process can also be initiated manually using the System.GC type. Initiating a garbage collection freezes all threads in the process to allow the GC time to examine the managed heap.

The GC begins with the set of object references considered *roots* and walks the object graph, marking all the objects it touches as reachable. Once this process is complete, all objects that have not been marked are considered to be garbage.

Objects that are considered garbage and that don't have finalizers are immediately discarded, and the memory is reclaimed. Objects that are considered garbage and that do have finalizers are flagged for additional asynchronous processing on a separate thread to invoke their Finalize methods before they can be considered garbage and reclaimed at the next collection.

Objects considered still live are then shifted down to the bottom of the heap (*compacted*), hopefully freeing space to allow the memory allocation to succeed.

At this point the memory allocation is attempted again, the threads in the process are unfrozen, and either normal processing continues or an OutOfMemoryException is thrown.

Optimization Techniques

Although this may sound like an inefficient process compared to simply managing memory manually, the GC incorporates various optimization techniques to reduce the time an application is frozen waiting for the GC to complete (known as *pause time*).

The most important of these optimizations is what makes the GC generational. This techniques takes advantage of the fact that while many objects tend to be allocated and discarded rapidly, certain objects are long-lived and thus don't need to be traced during every collection.

Basically, the GC divides the managed heap into three *generations*. Objects that have just been allocated are considered to be in Gen0, objects that have survived one collection cycle are considered to be in Gen1, and all other objects are considered to be in Gen2.

When it performs a collection, the GC initially collects only Gen0 objects. If not enough memory is reclaimed to fulfill the request, both Gen0 and Gen1 objects are collected, and if that fails as well, a full collection of Gen0, Gen1, and Gen2 object is attempted.

Many other optimizations are also used to enhance the performance of automatic memory management, and in general a GC-based application can be expected to approach the performance of one using manual memory management.

Finalizers

When implementing your own types, you can choose to give them *finalizers*, which are methods called asynchronously by the GC once an object is determined to be garbage.

Although this is required in certain cases, in general there are many good technical reasons to avoid the use of finalizers.

As described in the previous section, objects with finalizers incur significant overhead when they are collected, requiring asynchronous invocation of their `Finalize` methods and taking two full GC cycles for their memory to be reclaimed.

Other reasons not to use finalizers include:

- Objects with finalizers take longer to allocate on the managed heap than objects without finalizers.

- Objects with finalizers that refer to other objects (even those without finalizers) can prolong the life of the referred objects unnecessarily.

- It's impossible to predict in what order the finalizers for a set of objects will be called.

- You have limited control over when (or even if!) the finalizer for an object will be called.

In summary, finalizers are somewhat like lawyers: while there are cases where you really need them, in general you don't want to use them unless absolutely necessary, and if you do use them, you need to be 100% sure you understand what they are doing for you.

If you have to implement a finalizer, follow these guidelines or have a very good reason for not doing so:

- Ensure that your finalizer executes quickly.

- Never block in your finalizer.

- Free any unmanaged resources you own.

- Don't reference any other objects.

- Don't throw any unhandled exceptions.

- Call the `Finalize` method of the base class before returning.

Dispose and Close Methods

It is generally desirable to explicitly call clean-up code once you have determined that an object will no longer be used. Microsoft recommends that you write a method named either `Dispose` or `Close` (depending on the semantics of the type) to perform the cleanup required. If you also have a `Finalize` method, include a special call to the static `Suppress-Finalize` method on the `System.GC` type to indicate that the `Finalize` method no longer needs to be called. Typically the real `Finalize` method is written to call the `Dispose/Close` method, as follows:

```
public class Worker {
  ...
  public void Dispose() {
    // Perform normal cleanup
    ...
    // Mark this object finalized
    GC.SuppressFinalize(this);
  }
  protected override void Finalize() {
    Dispose();
    base.Finalize();
  }
}
```

Interop with Native DLLs

PInvoke, short for Platform Invocation Services, lets C# access functions, structs, and callbacks in unmanaged DLLs. For example, perhaps you wish to call the `MessageBox` function in the Windows `user32.dll`:

```
int MessageBox(HWND hWnd, LPCTSTR lpText,
            LPCTSTR lpCation, UINT uType);
```

To call this function, you can write a **static extern** method decorated with the **DllImport** attribute:

```
using System.Runtime.InteropServices;
[DllImport("user32.dll")]
static extern int MessageBox(int hWnd, string text,
                            string caption, int type);
```

PInvoke then finds and loads the required Win32 DLLs and resolves the entry point of the requested function. The CLR includes a marshaler that knows how to convert parameters and return values between .NET types and unmanaged types. In this example the **int** parameters translate directly to four-byte integers that the function expects, and the **string** parameters are converted to null-terminated arrays of characters using one-byte ANSI characters under Win9x or two-byte Unicode characters under WinNT/Win2K.

Marshaling Common Types

The CLR marshaler is a .NET facility that knows about the core types used by COM and the Windows API and provides default translations to CLR types for you. The **bool** type, for instance, can be translated into a two-byte Windows **BOOL** type or a four-byte **Boolean** type. You can override a default translation using the **MarshalAs** attribute:

```
using System.Runtime.InteropServices;
static extern int Foo([MarshalAs(UnmanagedType.LPStr)]
                      string s);
```

In this case, the marshaler was told to use **LPStr**, so it will always use ANSI characters. Array classes and the **StringBuilder** class will copy the marshaled value from an external function back to the managed value, as follows:

```
using System.Runtime.InteropServices;
[DllImport("kernel32.dll")]
static extern int GetWindowsDirectory(StringBuilder sb,
                                      int maxChars);
class Test {
    static void Main() {
        StringBuilder s = new String(256);
        GetWindowsDirectory(s, 256);
        Console.WriteLine(s);
    }
}
```

Marshaling Classes and Structs

Passing a class or struct to a C function requires marking the struct or class with the **StructLayout** attribute:

```
using System.Runtime.InteropServices;
[StructLayout(LayoutKind.Sequential)]
class SystemTime {
    public ushort wYear;
    public ushort wMonth;
    public ushort wDayOfWeek;
    public ushort wDay;
    public ushort wHour;
    public ushort wMinute;
    public ushort wSecond;
    public ushort wMilliseconds;
}
class Test {
    [DllImport("kernel32.dll")]
    static extern void GetSystemTime(SystemTime t);
    static void Main() {
        SystemTime t = new SystemTime();
        GetSystemTime(t);
        Console.WriteLine(t.wYear);
    }
}
```

In both C and C#, fields in an object are located at n number of bytes from the address of that object. The difference is that a C# program finds this offset by looking it up using the field name; C field names are compiled directly into offsets. For instance, in C, **wDay** is just a token to represent whatever is at the address of a **SystemTime** instance plus 24 bytes.

For access speed and future widening of a datatype, these offsets are usually in multiples of a minimum width, called the *pack size*. For .NET types, the pack size is usually set at the discretion of the runtime, but by using the **StructLayout** attribute, field offsets can be controlled. The default pack size when using this attribute is 8 bytes, but it can be set to 1, 2, 4, 8, or 16 bytes, and there are also explicit options to control individual field offsets. This lets a .NET type be passed to a C function.

In and Out Marshaling

The previous **Test** example works if **SystemTime** is a struct and **t** is a **ref** parameter, but is actually less efficient:

```
struct SystemTime {...}
static extern void GetSystemTime(ref SystemTime t);
```

This is because the marshaler must always create fresh values for external parameters, so the previous method copies t when going in to the function and then copies the marshaled t when coming out of the function. By default, pass-by-value parameters are copied in, C# ref parameters are copied in/out, and C# out parameters are copied out, but there are exceptions for the types that have custom conversions. For instance, array classes and the **StringBuilder** class require copying when coming out of a function, so they are in/out. It is occasionally useful to override this behavior, with the in and out attributes. For example, if an array should be read-only, the in modifier indicates to only copy the array going into the function, and not coming out of it:

```
static extern void Foo([in] int[] array);
```

Callbacks from Unmanaged Code

C# can not only call C functions but can also be called by C functions, using callbacks. In C# a **delegate** type is used in place of a function pointer:

```
class Test {
    delegate bool CallBack(int hWnd, int lParam);
    [DllImport("user32.dll")]
    static extern int EnumWindows(CallBack hWnd, int lParam);
    static bool PrintWindow(int hWnd, int lParam) {
        Console.WriteLine(hWnd);
        return true;
    }
    static void Main() {
        CallBack e = new CallBack(PrintWindow);
        EnumWindows(e, 0);
    }
}
```

Predefined Interop Support Attributes

The BCL provides a set of attributes you can use to mark up your objects with information that is used by the CLR marshaling services to alter their default marshaling behavior.

This section describes the most common attributes you will need when interoperating with native Win32 DLLs. These attributes all exist in the **System.Runtime.InteropServices** namespace.

DllImport attribute

```
[DllImport (dll-name
    [, EntryPoint=function-name]?
    [, CharSet=charset-enum]?
    [, SetLastError=true|false]?
    [, ExactSpelling=true|false]?
    [, CallingConvention=callconv-enum]?)]
```
(for methods)

The DllImport attribute annotates an external function that defines a DLL entry point. The parameters for this attribute are:

dll-name

A string specifying the name of the DLL.

function-name

A string specifying the function name in the DLL. This is useful if you want the name of your C# function to be different from the name of the DLL function.

charset-enum

A CharSet enum, specifying how to marshal strings. The default value is CharSet.Auto, which converts strings to ANSI characters on Win98, and Unicode characters on WinNT.

SetLastError

If true, preserves the Win32 error info. The default is false.

ExactSpelling

If true, the EntryPoint must exactly match the function. If false, name-matching heuristics are used. The default is false.

callconv-enum

A CallingConvention enum, specifying the mode to use with the EntryPoint. Default is StdCall.

StructLayout attribute

```
[StructLayout(layout-enum
    [, Pack=packing-size]?
    [, CharSet=charset-enum]?
  [, CheckFastMarshal=[true|false])?]
```
(for classes, structs)

The StructLayout attribute specifies how the data members of a class or struct should be laid out in memory. Although this attribute is commonly used when declaring structures that are passed to or returned from native

DLLs, it can also define data structures suited to file and network I/O. The parameters for this attribute are:

layout-enum

> A LayoutKind enum, which can be 1) *sequential*, which lays out fields one after the next with a minimum pack size; 2) *union*, which makes all fields have an offset of 0, so long as they are value types; 3) *explicit*, which lets each field have a custom offset.

packing-size

> An int specifying whether the packing size is 1, 2, 4, 8, or 16 bytes. The default value is 8.

charset-enum

> A CharSet enum, specifying how to marshal strings. The default value is CharSet.Auto, which converts strings to ANSI characters on Win98, and Unicode characters on WinNT.

CheckFastMarshal

> A Boolean value specifying whether a compile-time warning should be generated if the type isn't block transferable ("blittable"). The default is false.

FieldOffset attribute

> [FieldOffset (*byte-offset*)] (for fields)

The FieldOffset attribute is used within a class or struct that has explicit field layout. This attribute can be applied to a field and specifies the field offset in bytes from the start of the class or struct. Note that these offsets don't have to be strictly increasing and can overlap, thus creating a union data structure.

MarshalAs attribute

> [MarshalAs(*unmanaged-type*)
>   [, *named-parameters*]?]
> (for fields, parameters, return values)

The MarshalAs attribute overrides the default marshaling behavior the marshaler applies to a parameter or field. The *unmanaged-type* value is taken from the UnmanagedType enum; see the following list for the permissible values:

Bool	LPStr	VBByRefStr
I1	LPWStr	AnsiBStr
U1	LPTStr	TBStr

I2	ByValTStr	VariantBool
U2	Iunknown	FunctionPtr
I4	Idispatch	LPVoid
U4	Struct	AsAny
I8	Interface	RPrecise
U8	SafeArray	LPArray
R4	ByValArray	LPStruct
R8	SysInt	CustomMarshaler
BStr	SysUInt	NativeTypeMax
Error		

For a detailed description of how and when to use each of these enum values, as well as other legal *named-parameters*, see the .NET Framework SDK documentation.

In attribute

[In] (for parameters)

The In attribute specifies that data should be marshaled into the caller and can be combined with the Out attribute.

Out attribute

[Out] (for parameters)

The Out attribute specifies that data should be marshaled out from the called method to the caller and can be combined with the In attribute.

Interop with COM

The CLR provides support both for exposing C# objects as COM objects and for using COM objects from C#.

Binding COM and C# Objects

Interoperating between COM and C# works through either early or late binding. Early binding allows you to program with types known at compile time, while late binding forces you to program with types via dynamic discovery, using reflection on the C# side and IDispatch on the COM side.

When calling COM programs from C#, early binding works by providing metadata in the form of an assembly for the COM object and its interfaces. *TlbImp.exe* takes a COM type library and generates the equivalent metadata in an assembly. With the generated assembly, it's possible to instantiate and call methods on a COM object just as you would on any other C# object.

When calling C# programs from COM, early binding works via a type library. Both *TlbExp.exe* and *RegAsm.exe* allow you to generate a COM type library from your assembly. You can then use this type library with tools that support early binding via type libraries such as Visual Basic 6.

Exposing COM Objects to C#

When you instantiate a COM object you are actually working with a proxy known as the Runtime Callable Wrapper (RCW). The RCW is responsible for managing the lifetime requirements of the COM object and translating the methods called on it into the appropriate calls on the COM object. When the garbage collector finalizes the RCW, it releases all references to the object it was holding. For situations where you need to release the COM object without waiting for the garbage collector to finalize the RCW, you can use the static `ReleaseComObject` method of the `System.Runtime.InteropServices.Marshal` type.

The following example demonstrates adding a contact to MSN Instant Messenger from C# via COM Interop:

```
// IMAdd.cs - compile with /r:Messenger.dll
// Run IMAdd.exe <UserID> to add an MSN Instant
//    Messenger user to Contacts
// Run TlbImp.exe "C:\Program Files\Messenger\msmsgs.exe"
//    to create Messenger.dll
using System.Runtime.InteropServices;
using Messenger; // COM API for MSN Instant Messenger
class COMConsumer {
    static void Main(string[] args) {
        MessengerApp m = new MessengerApp()
        m.LaunchAddContactUI(args[0]);
    }
}
```

Exposing C# Objects to COM

Just as an RCW proxy wraps a COM object when you access it from C#, code that accesses a C# object as a COM object must do so through a proxy as well. When your C# object is marshaled out to COM, the runtime creates a COM Callable Wrapper (CCW). The CCW follows the same lifetime rules as other COM objects, and as long as it is alive, a CCW maintains a traceable reference to the object it wraps, which keeps the object alive when the garbage collector is run.

The following example shows how you can export both a class and an interface from C# and control the Global Unique Identifiers (GUIDs) and Dispatch IDs (DISPIDs) assigned. After compiling `IRunInfo` and `Stack-Snapshot` you can register both using *RegAsm.exe.*

```
[GuidAttribute("aa6b10a2-dc4f-4a24-ae5e-90362c2142c1")]
public interface : IRunInfo {
  [DispId(1)]
  string GetRunInfo();
}
[GuidAttribute("b72ccf55-88cc-4657-8577-72bd0ff767bc")]
public class StackSnapshot : IRunInfo {
  public StackSnapshot() {
    st = new StackTrace();
  }
  [DispId(1)]
  public string GetRunInfo() {
    return st.ToString();
  }
  private StackTrace st;
}
```

COM Mapping in C#

When you use a COM object from C#, the RCW makes a COM method look like a normal C# instance method. In COM, methods normally return an HRESULT to indicate success or failure and use an out parameter to return a value. In C#, however, methods normally return their result values and use exceptions to report errors. The RCW handles this by checking the HRESULT returned from the call to a COM method and throwing a C# exception when it finds a failure result. With a success result, the RCW returns the parameter marked as the return value in the COM method signature.

 For more information on the argument modifiers and default mappings from COM type library types to C# types, see Appendix D, *Data Marshaling.*

Common COM Interop Support Attributes

The BCL provides a set of attributes you can use to mark up your objects with information needed by the CLR interop services to expose managed types to the unmanaged world as COM objects.

This section describes the most common attributes you will use for this purpose. These attributes all exist in the `System.Runtime.Interop-Services` namespace.

ComVisible attribute

```
[ComVisible(true|false)]
```
(for assemblies, classes, structs, enums, interfaces, delegates)

When generating a type library, all public types in an assembly are exported by default. The `ComVisible` attribute specifies that particular public types (or even the entire assembly) should not be exposed.

DispId attribute

```
[DispId(dispatch-id)]
```
(for methods, properties, fields)

The `DispId` attribute specifies the `DispID` assigned to a method, field, or property for access via an `IDispatch` interface.

ProgId attribute

```
[ProgId(progid)]
```
(for classes)

The `ProgId` attribute specifies the COM `ProgID` to be used for your class.

Guid attribute

```
[GuidAttribute(guid)]
```
(for assemblies, modules, classes, structs, enums, interfaces, delegates)

The `Guid` attribute specifies the COM GUID to be used for your class or interface. This attribute should be specified using its full type name to avoid clashes with the `Guid` type.

HasDefaultInterface attribute

```
[HasDefaultInterface]
```
(for classes)

The `HasDefaultInterface` attribute specifies that the first inherited interface on the class should be used as the default interface (instead of generating a unique interface).

InterfaceType attribute

```
[InterfaceType(ComInterfaceType)]
```
(for interfaces)

By default, interfaces are generated as dual interfaces in the type library, but you can use this attribute to one of the three COM interface types (dual, dispatch, or a traditional `IUnknown`-derived interface).

ComRegisterFunction attribute

[ComRegisterFunction] (for methods)

Requests that *RegAsm.exe* call a method during the process of registering your assembly.

NoIDispatch attribute

[NoIDispatch] (for classes)

The `NoIDispatch` attribute specifies that a request for `IID_IDispatch` for the class should return `E_NOINTERFACE`.

4

Base Class Library Overview

In Chapter 3, *Programming the .NET Framework*, we focused on some of the key aspects of the .NET Framework and how to leverage them from C#. However, access to these capabilities isn't limited to C#.

Almost all the capabilities of the .NET Framework are exposed via a set of managed types known as the Base Class Library (BCL). Because these types are CLS-compliant, they are accessible from almost any .NET language. BCL types are grouped logically by namespace and are exported from a set of assemblies (DLLs) that are part of the .NET platform. Using these types in a C# application requires you to reference the appropriate assembly when compiling (see Appendix F, *Namespaces and Assemblies*).

In order to work effectively in C# on the .NET platform, it is important to understand the general capabilities in the predefined class library. However, the library is far too large to cover completely in this book, as it encompasses approximately 4,500 types grouped into 120 namespaces and exported from 40 different assemblies.

Instead, in this chapter, we give an overview of the entire BCL (broken down by logical area) and provide references to relevant types and namespaces so that you can explore their details in the .NET Framework SDK on your own.

The specific types and namespaces mentioned in this overview are based on beta 1 of the .NET Framework and may change in future betas and the released version.

Some namespaces and types listed here aren't documented, and are therefore unsupported by Microsoft. For clarity, these namespaces are listed in `constant width italics`.

Useful tools for exploring the BCL include the .NET Framework SDK documentation, the *WinCV.exe* class browser, and the *ILAsm.exe* disassembler (see Chapter 5, *Essential .NET Tools*)

Core Types

The core types are contained in the **System** namespace. This namespace is the heart of the BCL and contains classes, interfaces, and attributes that all other types depend on. The root of the BCL is the type **Object**, from which all other .NET types derive. Other fundamental types are **Value-Type** (base type for structs), **Enum** (base type for enums), **Convert** (used to convert between base types), **Exception** (base type for all exceptions), and the boxed versions of the predefined value types. Interfaces that are used throughout the BCL such as **ICloneable**, **IComparable**, **IFormattable**, and **IConvertible** are defined here (see "Strings" in Chapter 3). Extended types such as **DateTime**, **TimeSpan**, and **DBNull** are also available. Other classes include support for single and multicast delegates (see "Delegates" in Chapter 2, *C# Language Reference*), basic math operations (see "Math" in Chapter 3), attributes (see "Attributes" in Chapter 2), and exception handling (see "try Statements and Exceptions" in Chapter 2).

For more string information, see the **String** namespace.

Text

The BCL provides rich support for text. Important types include a **String** class for handling immutable strings, a **StringBuilder** class that provides string-handling operations with support for locale-aware comparison operations and multiple string encoding formats (ASCII, Unicode, UTF-7, and UTF-8), and a set of classes that provide regular expression support (see "Strings" in Chapter 3).

```
System.Text
System.Text.RegularExpressions
```

Important types in other namespaces include **System.String**.

Collections

The BCL provides a set of general-purpose data structures such as **Array-List**, **Dictionary**, **Hashtable**, **Queue**, **Stack**, **BitArray**, and more.

Standardized design patterns using common base types and public interfaces allow consistent handling of collections throughout the BCL for both pre-defined and user-defined collection types (see "Collections" in Chapter 3).

For more information, see the following namespaces:

```
System.Collections
System.Collections.Bases
```

Important types in other namespaces include **System.Array**.

Streams and I/O

The BCL provides good support for accessing the standard input, output and error streams. Classes are also provided for performing binary and text file I/O, registering for notification of file system events, and for accessing a secure user-specific storage area known as Isolated Storage (see "Input/Output" in Chapter 3).

For more information, see the following namespaces:

```
System.IO
System.IO.IsolatedStorage
System.Console
```

Networking

The BCL provides a layered set of classes for communicating over the network using different levels of abstraction including raw socket access; TCP, UDP, and HTTP protocol support; a high-level request/response mechanism based on URIs and streams; and pluggable protocol handlers (see "Networking" in Chapter 3).

For more information, see the following namespaces:

```
System.Net
System.Net.Sockets
```

Important types in other namespaces include **System.IO.Stream**.

Threading

The BCL provides rich support for building multithreaded applications, including thread and thread pool management; thread-synchronization mechanisms such as monitors, mutexes, events, reader/writer locks, etc.; and access to such underlying platform features as I/O completion ports and system timers (see "Threading" in Chapter 3).

For more information, see the following namespaces:

```
System.Threading
System.Timers
System.Timers.Design
```

Important types in other namespaces include **System.Thread-StaticAttribute.**

Security

The BCL provides classes for manipulating all elements of the .NET runtime's Code Access Security model, including security policies, security principals, permission sets, and evidence. These classes also support cryptographic algorithms such as DES, 3DES, RC2, RSA, DSig, MD5, SHA1, and Base64 encoding for stream transformations.

For more information, see the following namespaces:

```
System.Security
System.Security.Cryptography
System.Security.Cryptography.X509Certificates
System.Security.Cryptography.Xml
System.Security.Permissions
System.Security.Policy
System.Security.Principal
```

Reflection

The .NET runtime depends heavily on the existence of metadata and the ability to inspect and manipulate it dynamically. The BCL exposes this via a set of abstract classes that mirror the significant elements of an application (assemblies, modules, types, and members) and provide support for creating instances of BCL types and new types on the fly (see "Reflection" in Chapter 3).

For more information, see the following namespaces:

```
System.Reflection
System.Reflection.Emit
```

Important types in other namespaces include:

```
System.Type
System. Activator
System.AppDomain.
```

Serialization

The BCL includes support for serializing arbitrary object graphs to and from a stream. This serialization can store and transmit complex data structures via files or the network. The default serializers provide binary and XML-based formatting but can be extended with user-defined formatters.

For more information, see the following namespaces:

```
System.Runtime.Serialization
System.Runtime.Serialization.Formatters
System.Runtime.Serialization.Formatters.Soap
System.Runtime.Serialization.Formatters.Binary
```

Important types in other namespaces include:

```
System.NonSerializedAttribute
System.SerializableAttribute
```

Remoting

Remoting is the cornerstone of a distributed application, and the BCL provides excellent support for making and receiving remote method calls. Calls may be synchronous or asynchronous; support request/response or one-way modes; can be delivered over multiple transports (TCP, HTTP, and SMTP); and can be serialized in multiple formats (SOAP and binary). The remoting infrastructure supports multiple activation models, lease-based object lifetimes, distributed object identity, object marshaling by reference and by value, and message interception. These types can be extended with user-defined channels, serializers, proxies, and call context.

For more information, see the following namespaces:

```
System.Runtime.Remoting
System.Runtime.Remoting.Channels.Core
System.Runtime.Remoting.Channels.HTTP
System.Runtime.Remoting.Channels.MetadataServices
System.Runtime.Remoting.Channels.SMTP
System.Runtime.Remoting.Channels.TCP
System.Runtime.Remoting.Services
```

Important types in other namespaces include:

```
System.AppDomain
System.CallContext
System.ContextBoundObject
System.ContextStaticAttribute
System.MarshalByRefObject
```

Web Services

Logically, web services are simply an instance of remoting. In reality, the BCL support for web services is considered part of ASP .NET and is largely separate from the CLR remoting infrastructure. Classes and attributes exist for describing and publishing web services, discovering what web services are exposed at a particular endpoint (URI), and invoking a web service method.

For more information, see the following namespaces:

```
System.Web.Services
System.Web.Services.Description
System.Web.Services.Discovery
System.Web.Services.Interop
System.Web.Services.Protocols
```

Data Access

The BCL includes a set of classes that access data sources and manage complex data sets. Known as ADO .NET, these classes are the managed replacement for ADO under Win32. ADO+ supports both connected and disconnected operations, multiple data providers (including nonrelational data sources), and serialization to and from XML.

For more information, see the following namespaces:

```
System.Data
System.Data.ADO
System.Data.ADO.Interop
System.Data.CodeGen
System.Data.Design
System.Data.Internal
System.Data.SQL
System.Data.SQLTypes
```

XML

The BCL provides broad support for XML 1.0, XML schemas, and XML namespaces, with two separate XML parsing models (a DOM2-based model and a pull-mode variant of SAX2) and implementations of XSL/T, XPath, and SOAP 1.1.

For more information, see the following namespaces:

```
System.Xml
System.Xml.Serialization
System.Xml.Serialization.IO
System.Xml.Serialization.Schema
```

```
System.Xml.XPath
System.Xml.Xsl
```

Graphics

The BCL includes classes to support working with graphic images. Known as GDI+, these classes are the managed equivalent of GDI under Win32, and include support for brushes, fonts, bitmaps, text rendering, drawing primitives, image conversions, and print-preview capabilities.

For more information, see the following namespaces:

```
System.Drawing
System.Drawing.Design
System.Drawing.Drawing2D
System.Drawing.Imaging
System.Drawing.Printing
System.Drawing.Text
```

Rich Client Applications

The BCL includes support for creating classic GUI applications. This support is called Windows Forms and consists of a forms package, a predefined set of GUI components, and a component model suited to RAD designer tools. These classes provide varying degrees of abstraction from low-level message-loop handler classes to high-level layout managers and visual inheritance.

For more information, see the following namespaces:

```
System.WinForms
System.WinForms.ComponentModel
System.WinForms.ComponentModel.COM2Interop
System.WinForms.Design
System.WinForms.PropertyGridInternal
```

Web-Based Applications

The BCL includes support for creating web-based applications. This support is called *Web Forms* and consists of a server-side forms package that generates HTML UI, a predefined set of HTML-based GUI widgets, and a component model suited to RAD designer tools. The BCL also includes a set of classes that manage session state, security, caching, debugging, tracing, localization, configuration, and deployment for web-based applications. Finally, the BCL includes the classes and attributes that produce and consume web services, which were described previously in the "Web Services" section. Collectively, these capabilities are known as ASP .NET and are a complete replacement for ASP under Win32.

For more information, see the following namespaces:

```
System.Web
System.Web.Caching
System.Web.Configuration
System.Web.Handlers
System.Web.Hosting
System.Web.Security
System.Web.SessionState
System.Web.UI
System.Web.UI.Design
System.Web.UI.Design.Util
System.Web.UI.Design.WebControls
System.Web.UI.Design.WebControls.ListControls
System.Web.UI.HtmlControls
System.Web.UI.WebControls
System.Web.UI.WebControls.Design
System.Web.Util
```

Globalization

The BCL provides classes that aid globalization by supporting code-page conversions, locale-aware string operations, date/time conversions, and the use of resource files to centralize localization work.

For more information, see the following namespaces:

```
System.Globalization
System.Resources
```

Configuration

The BCL provides access to the .NET configuration system, which includes a per-user and per-application configuration model with inheritance of configuration settings, and a transacted installer framework. Classes exist both to use the configuration framework and to extend it.

For more information, see the following namespaces:

```
System.Configuration
System.Configuration.Assemblies
System.Configuration.Core
System.Configuration.Design
System.Configuration.Install
System.Configuration.Interceptors
System.Configuration.Internal
System.Configuration.Schema
System.Configuration.Web
```

Advanced Component Services

The BCL provides support for building on the COM+ services such as distributed transactions, JIT activation, object pooling, queuing, and events. The BCL also includes types that provide access to reliable, asynchronous, one-way messaging via an existing Message Queue infrastructure (MSMQ). The BCL also includes classes that provide access to existing directory services (Active Directory).

For more information, see the following namespaces:

```
Microsoft.ComServices
System.DirectoryServices
System.Messaging
System.Messaging.Design
```

Assemblies

The BCL provides attributes that tag the metadata on an assembly with information such as target OS and processor, assembly version, and other information.

For more information, see the following namespaces:

```
System.Runtime.CompilerServices
System.Runtime.CompilerServices.CSharp
```

Diagnostics and Debugging

The BCL includes classes that provide debug tracing with multilistener support; access to the event log; access to process, thread, and stack frame information; and the ability to create and consume performance counters.

For more information, see the following namespaces:

```
System.Diagnostics
System.Diagnostics.Design
System.Diagnostics.SymbolStore
```

Interoperating with Unmanaged Code

The .NET runtime supports bidirectional interop with unmanaged code via COM, COM+, and native Win32 API calls. The BCL provides a set of classes and attributes that support this, including precise control of managed object lifetime, and the option of creating user-defined custom marshallers to handle specific interop situations.

For more information, see the following namespaces:

```
System.Runtime.InteropServices
System.Runtime.InteropServices.CustomMarshalers
System.Runtime.InteropServices.Expando
Microsoft.Win32.Interop
Microsoft.Win32.Interop.Trident
```

Important types in other namespaces include System.Buffer.

Component and Tool Support

In the .NET runtime, components are distinguished from classes by the presence of additional metadata and other apparatus that facilitates the use of the component forms packages such as Windows Forms and Web Forms. The BCL provides classes and attributes that support both the creation of components and the creation of tools that consume components. These classes also include the ability to generate and compile C#, JScript, and VB.NET source code.

For more information, see the following namespaces:

```
System.CodeDOM
System.CodeDOM.Compiler
System.ComponentModel
System.ComponentModel.Design
System.ComponentModel.Design.CodeModel
System.ComponentModel.Interop
```

Runtime Facilities

The BCL provides classes that can control runtime behavior. The canonical examples are the classes that control the garbage collector and those that provide strong and weak reference support.

For more information, see the System namespace.

Important types in other namespaces include System.Runtime.InteropServices.GCHandle.

Native OS Facilities

The BCL provides support for controlling existing NT services and creating new ones. It also provides access to certain native Win32 facilities such as the Windows registry and the Windows Management Instrumentation (WMI).

For more information, see the following namespaces:

```
Accessibility
Microsoft.Win32
System.Core
System.Management
System.ServiceProcess
```

5

Essential .NET Tools

The .NET Framework SDK contains many useful programming tools. Here, in an alphabetical list, are those we have found most useful or necessary for developing C# applications. Unless otherwise noted, the tools in this list can all be found in the *bin* directory of your .NET Framework SDK installation, but once the .NET Framework is installed, you can access them from any directory. To use any of these tools, invoke a Command Prompt window and enter the name of the desired tool. For a complete list of the available command-line switches for any given tool, enter the tool name (e.g., **csc**) and press the Return key.

ADepends.exe: assembly dependency list

Adepends displays all assemblies that a given assembly is dependent on to load. This is a useful C# program found among the samples in the *tool developers guide* directory of the .NET Framework directory tree. You need to install these samples before you can use them, because they are not installed by default.

Al.exe: assembly linking utility

Creates an assembly manifest from the modules and resources files you name. You can also include Win32 resources files. Here's an example:

```
al /out:c.dll a.dll b.dll
```

CorDbg.exe: runtime debugger

General source level command line debug utility for MSIL programs. Very useful tool for C# source debugging. Source for *cordbg* is available in the *tool developers guide* directory.

Csc.exe: C# compiler

Compiles C# sources, and incorporates resource files and separately compiled modules. Also allows you to specify conditional compilation options, XML documentation, and path information. Here are some examples:

```
csc foo.cs /r:bar.dll /win32res:foo.res
csc foo.cs /debug /define:TEMP
```

DbgUrt.exe: GUI debugger

Windows-based source level debugger. Available in the *GuiDebug* directory of the .NET Framework SDK installation.

GACUtil.exe: global assembly cache utility

Allows you to install, uninstall, and list the contents of the global assembly cache. Here's an example:

```
gacutil /i c.dll
```

ILAsm.exe: MSIL assembler

Creates MSIL modules and assemblies directly from an MSIL textual representation.

ILDasm.exe: MSIL disassembler

Disassembles modules and assemblies. The default is to display a tree style representation, but you can also specify an output file. Here are some examples:

```
ildasm b.dll
ildasm b.dll /out=b.asm
```

InstalUtil.exe: installer utility

Executes installers and uninstallers contained within the assembly. A logfile can be written, and state information can be persisted.

nmake.exe: make utility

Common utility that scripts building of multiple components and source files and tracks rebuild dependency information. See Appendix E, *Working with Assemblies*, for more information.

PEVerify.exe: portable executable verifier

Verifies that your compiler has generated type-safe MSIL. C# will always generates type-safe MSIL. Useful interop with ILASM-based programs.

RegAsm.exe: register assembly tool

Registers an assembly in the system registry. This allows COM clients to call managed methods. You can also use it to generate the registry file, for future registration. Here's an example:

```
regasm /regfile:c.reg c.dll
```

RegSvcs.exe: register services utility

Registers an assembly to COM+ 1.0, and installs its typelib into an existing application. Can also generate a typelib. Here's an example:

```
regsvcs foo.dll comapp newfoo.tlb
```

Sn.exe: shared name utility

Verifies assemblies and their key information. Also generates key files. Here's an example:

```
sn -k mykey.snk
```

SoapSuds.exe: SoapSuds utility

Creates XML schemas for services in an assembly and creates assemblies from a schema. You can also reference the schema via its URL. Here's an example:

```
soapsuds
   -url:http://localhost/myapp/app.soap?SDL
   -os:app.xml
```

TlbExp.exe: type library exporter

Exports a COM typelib derived from the public types within the supplied assembly. Differs from *regasm* in that it doesn't perform any registration. Here's an example:

```
tlbexp /out:c.tlb c.dll
```

TlbImp.exe: type library importer

Creates a managed assembly from the supplied COM typelib, mapping the type definitions to .NET types. You need to import this new assembly into your C# program for use. Here's an example:

```
tlbimp /out:MyOldCom.dll MyCom.tlb
```

WebServiceUtil.exe: web service utility

Creates service descriptions and generates proxies for ASP .NET web-service methods. See the ASP.NET documentation in the .NET Framework SDK for more detail on web services.

WinCV.exe: windows class viewer

Searches for matching names within a supplied assembly. If none are supplied, it uses the default libraries. The namespaces and classes are displayed in a listbox, and the selected type information displays in another window.

WinDes.exe: windows designer

A WinForms-based component designer for C# or Visual Basic forms with toolbox, property editor, and a display form.

Xsd.exe: XML schema definition tool

Generates XML schemas from XDR, XML files, or class information. Also can generate DataSet or class information from a schema. Here's an example:

```
xsd foo.xdr
xsd bar.dll
```

C# Keywords

abstract

A class modifier that specifies that the class must be derived-from to be instantiated.

as

A binary operator type that casts the left operand to the type specified by the right operand and that returns `null` rather than throwing an exception if the cast fails.

base

A variable with the same meaning as `this`, except it accesses a base class implementation of a member.

bool

A logical datatype that can be `true` or `false`.

break

A jump statement that exits a loop or `switch` statement block.

byte

A one-byte unsigned integral datatype.

case

A selection statement that defines a particular choice in a `switch` statement.

catch

The part of a `try` statement that catches exceptions of a specific type defined in the `catch` clause.

char

A two-byte Unicode character datatype.

checked
>   A statement or operator that enforces arithmetic bounds checking on an expression or statement block.

class
>   An extendable reference type that combines data and functionality into one unit.

const
>   A modifier for a local variable or field declaration that indicates the value is a constant. A const that is evaluated at compile time and can only be a predefined type.

continue
>   A jump statement that skips the remaining statements in a statement block and continues to the next iteration in a loop.

decimal
>   A twelve-byte precise decimal datatype.

default
>   A marker in a switch statement specifying the action to take when no case statements match the switch expression.

delegate
>   A type for defining a method signature, so that delegate instances can hold and invoke a method or list of methods that match its signature.

do
>   A loop statement to iterate a statement block until an expression at the end of the loop evaluates to false.

double
>   An eight-byte floating-point datatype.

else
>   A conditional statement that defines the action to take when a preceding if expression evaluates to false.

enum
>   A value type that defines a group of named numeric constants.

event
>   A member modifier for a delegate field or property that indicates only the += and -= methods of the delegate can be accessed.

explicit
>   An operator that defines an explicit conversion.

extern

A method modifier that indicates the method is implemented with unmanaged code.

false

A Boolean literal.

finally

The part of a try statement to always execute when control leaves the scope of the try block.

fixed

A statement to pin down a reference type so that the garbage collector won't move it during pointer arithmetic operations.

float

A four-byte floating-point datatype.

for

A loop statement that combines an initialization statement, stopping condition, and iterative statement into one statement.

foreach

A loop statement that iterates over collections that implement IEnumerable.

get

The name of the accessor that returns the value of a property.

goto

A jump statement that jumps to a label within the same method and same scope as the jump point.

if

A conditional statement that executes its statement block if its expression evaluates to true.

implicit

An operator that defines an implicit conversion.

in

The operator between a type and an IEnumerable in a foreach statement.

int

A four-byte signed integral datatype.

interface

A contract that specifies the members that a class or struct may implement to receive generic services for that type.

internal
> An access modifier that indicates a type or type member is accessible only to other types in the same assembly.

is
> A relational operator that evaluates to true if the left operand's type matches, is derived from, or implements the type specified by the right operand.

lock
> A statement that acquires a lock on a reference-type object to help multiple threads cooperate.

long
> An eight-byte signed integral datatype.

namespace
> A keyword that maps a set of types to a common name.

new
> An operator that calls a constructor on a type, allocating a new object on the heap if the type is a reference type, or initializing the object if the type is a value type. The keyword is overloaded to hide an inherited member.

null
> A reference-type literal that indicates no object is referenced.

object
> The type all other types derive from.

operator
> A method modifier that overloads operators.

out
> A parameter modifier that specifies the parameter is passed by reference and must be assigned by the method being called.

override
> A method modifier that indicates that a method of a class overrides a virtual method of a class or interface.

params
> A parameter modifier that specifies that the last parameter of a method may accept multiple parameters of the same type.

private
> An access modifier that indicates that only the containing type can access the member.

protected

An access modifier that indicates that only the containing type or derived types can access the member.

public

An access modifier that indicates that a type or type member is accessible to all other types.

readonly

A field modifier specifying that a field can be assigned only once, either in its declaration or its containing type's constructor.

ref

A parameter modifier that specifies that the parameter is passed by reference and is assigned before being passed to the method.

return

A jump statement that exits a method, specifying a return value when the method is nonvoid.

sbyte

A one-byte signed integral datatype.

sealed

A class modifier that indicates a class cannot be derived-from.

set

The name of the accessor that sets the value of a property.

short

A two-byte signed integral datatype.

sizeof

An operator that returns the size in bytes of a struct.

stackalloc

An operator that returns a pointer to a specified number of value types allocated on the stack.

static

A type member modifier that indicates that the member applies to the type rather than an instance of the type.

string

A predefined reference type that represents an immutable sequence of Unicode characters.

struct

A value type that combines data and functionality in one unit.

switch
>   A selection statement that allows a selection of choices to be made based on the value of a predefined type.

this
>   A variable that references the current instance of a class or struct.

throw
>   A jump statement that throws an exception when an abnormal condition has occurred.

true
>   A Boolean literal.

try
>   A statement that provides a way to handle an exception or a premature exit in a statement block.

typeof
>   An operator that returns the type of an object as a System.Type object.

uint
>   A four-byte unsigned integral datatype.

ulong
>   An eight-byte unsigned integral datatype.

unchecked
>   A statement or operator that prevents arithmetic bounds checking on an expression.

unsafe
>   A method modifier or statement that permits pointer arithmetic to be performed within a particular block.

ushort
>   A two-byte unsigned integral datatype.

using
>   A keyword that specifies that types in a particular namespace can be referred to without requiring their fully qualified type names.

value
>   The name of the implicit variable set by the set accessor of a property.

virtual
>   A class method modifier that indicates that a method can be overridden by a derived class.

void

A keyword used in place of a type for methods that don't have a return value.

while

A loop statement to iterate a statement block while an expression at the start of each iteration evaluates to **false**.

B

Regular Expressions

The following tables summarize the regular-expression grammar and syntax supported by the regular-expression classes in **System.Text. RegularExpression**. Each of the modifiers and qualifiers in the tables can substantially change the behavior of the matching and searching patterns. For further information on regular expressions, we recommend the definitive *Mastering Regular Expressions* by Jeffrey E. F. Friedl (O'Reilly & Associates).

All the syntax described in the tables should match the Perl5 syntax, with specific exceptions noted.

Table B-1. Character Escapes

Escape Code Sequence	Meaning	Hexadecimal Equivalent
\a	Bell	\u0007
\b	Backspace	\u0008
\t	Tab	\u0009
\r	Carriage return	\u000A
\v	Vertical tab	\u000B
\f	Form feed	\u000C
\n	Newline	\u000D
\e	Escape	\u001B
\040	ASCII character as octal	
\x20	ASCII character as hex	
\cC	ASCII control character	

Table B-1. Character Escapes (continued)

Escape Code Sequence	Meaning	Hexadecimal Equivalent
\u0020	Unicode character as hex	
\non-escape	A nonescape character	

Special case: within a regular expression, \b means word boundary, except in a [] set, where \b means the backspace character.

Table B-2. Substitutions

Expression	Meaning
$group-number	Substitutes last substring matched by group-number
${group-name}	Substitutes last substring matched by (?<group-name>)

Substitutions are specified only within a replacement pattern.

Table B-3. Character Sets

Expression	Meaning
.	Matches any character except \n
[characterlist]	Matches a single character in the list
[^characterlist]	Matches a single character not in the list
[char0-char1]	Matches a single character in a range
\w	Matches a word character; same as [a-zA-Z_0-9]
\W	Matches a nonword character
\s	Matches a space character; same as [\n\r\t\f]
\S	Matches a nonspace character
\d	Matches a decimal digit; same as [0-9]
\D	Matches a nondigit

Table B-4. Positioning Assertions

Expression	Meaning
^	Beginning of line
$	End of line
\A	Beginning of string
\Z	End of line or string
\z	Exactly the end of string
\G	Where search started
\b	On a word boundary
\B	Not on a word boundary

Table B-5. Quantifiers

Quantifier	Meaning
*	0 or more matches
+	1 or more matches
?	0 or 1 matches
{n}	Exactly *n* matches
{n, }	At least *n* matches
{n,m}	At least *n*, but no more than *m* matches
*?	Lazy *, finds first match that has minimum repeats
+?	Lazy +, minimum repeats, but at least 1
??	Lazy ?, zero or minimum repeats
{n}?	Lazy {n}, exactly *n* matches
{n, }?	Lazy {n}, minimum repeats, but at least *n*
{n,m}?	Lazy {n,m}, minimum repeats, but at least *n*, and no more than *m*

Table B-6. Grouping Constructs

Syntax	Meaning
( )	Capture matched substring
(?<name>)	Capture matched substring into group *name*[a]
(?<number>)	Capture matched substring into group *number*[a]
(?<name1-name2>)	Undefine *name2*, and store interval and current group into *name1*; if *name2* is undefined, matching backtracks; *name1* is optional[a]
(?:)	Noncapturing group
(?imnsx-imnsx:)	Apply or disable matching options
(?=)	Continue matching only if subexpression matches on right
(?!)	Continue matching only if subexpression doesn't match on right
(?<=)	Continue matching only if subexpression matches on left[b]
(?<!)	Continue matching only if subexpression doesn't match on left[b]
(?>)	Subexpression is matched once, but isn't backtracked

[a] Single quotes may be used instead of angle brackets, for example (?'name').
[b] This construct doesn't backtrack; this is to remain compatible with Perl5.

The named capturing group syntax follows a suggestion made by Friedl in *Mastering Regular Expressions*. All other grouping constructs use the Perl5 syntax.

Table B-7. Back References

Parameter Syntax	Meaning
\count	Back reference *count* occurrences
\k<*name*>	Named back reference

Table B-8. Alternation

Expression Syntax	Meaning
|	Logical OR
(?(*expression*)yes|no)	Matches yes if expression matches, else no; the no is optional
(?(*name*)yes|no)	Matches yes if named string has a match, else no; the no is optional

Table B-9. Miscellaneous Constructs

Expression Syntax	Meaning
(?*imnsx-imnsx*)	Set or disable options in midpattern
(?#)	Inline comment
# [*to end of line*]	X-mode comment

Table B-10. Regular Expression Options

Option	Meaning
i	Case-insensitive match
m	Multiline mode; changes ^ and $ so they match beginning and ending of any line
n	Capture explicitly named or numbered groups
c	Compile to MSIL
s	Single-line mode; changes meaning of "." so it matches every character
x	Eliminates unescaped whitespace from the pattern
r	Search from right to left; can't be specified in midstream

C

Format Specifiers

Table C-1 lists the numeric format specifiers supported by the Format method on the predefined numeric types (see Chapter 3, *Programming the .NET Framework*).

Table C-1. Numeric Format Specifiers

Specifier	String Result	Datatype
C[*n*]	$XX,XX.XX ($XX,XXX.XX)	Currency
D[*n*]	[-]XXXXXXX	Decimal
E[*n*] or e[*n*]	[-]X.XXXXXXE+xxx [-]X.XXXXXXe+xxx [-]X.XXXXXXE-xxx [-]X.XXXXXXe-xxx	Exponent
F[*n*]	[-]XXXXXXX.XX	Fixed point
G[*n*]	General or scientific	General
N[*n*]	[-]XX,XXX.XX	Number
X[*n*] or x[*n*]	Hex representation	Hex

This is an example that uses numeric format specifiers without precision specifiers:

```
using System;
class TestDefaultFormats {
  static void Main() {
    int i = 654321;
    Console.WriteLine("{0:C}", i); // $654,321.00
    Console.WriteLine("{0:D}", i); // 654321
    Console.WriteLine("{0:E}", i); // 6.543210E+005
    Console.WriteLine("{0:F}", i); // 654321.00
```

```
      Console.WriteLine("{0:G}", i); // 654321
      Console.WriteLine("{0:N}", i); // 654,321.00
      Console.WriteLine("{0:X}", i); // 9FBF1
      Console.WriteLine("{0:x}", i); // 9fbf1
   }
}
```

This is an example that uses numeric format specifiers with precision specifiers on a variety of int values:

```
using System;
class TestIntegerFormats {
  static void Main() {
    int i = 123;
    Console.WriteLine("{0:C6}", i); // $123.000000
    Console.WriteLine("{0:D6}", i); // 000123
    Console.WriteLine("{0:E6}", i); // 1.230000E+002
    Console.WriteLine("{0:G6}", i); // 123
    Console.WriteLine("{0:N6}", i); // 123.000000
    Console.WriteLine("{0:X6}", i); // 00007B
    i = -123;
    Console.WriteLine("{0:C6}", i); // ($123.000000)
    Console.WriteLine("{0:D6}", i); // -000123
    Console.WriteLine("{0:E6}", i); // -1.230000E+002
    Console.WriteLine("{0:G6}", i); // -123
    Console.WriteLine("{0:N6}", i); // -123.000000
    Console.WriteLine("{0:X6}", i); // FFFF85
    i = 0;
    Console.WriteLine("{0:C6}", i); // $0.000000
    Console.WriteLine("{0:D6}", i); // 000000
    Console.WriteLine("{0:E6}", i); // 0.000000E+000
    Console.WriteLine("{0:G6}", i); // 0
    Console.WriteLine("{0:N6}", i); // 0.000000
    Console.WriteLine("{0:X6}", i); // 000000
  }
}
```

Here's an example that uses numeric format specifiers with precision specifiers on a variety of double values:

```
using System;
class TestDoubleFormats {
  static void Main() {
    double d = 1.23;
    Console.WriteLine("{0:C6}", d); // $1.230000
    Console.WriteLine("{0:E6}", d); // 1.230000E+000
    Console.WriteLine("{0:G6}", d); // 1.23
    Console.WriteLine("{0:N6}", d); // 1.230000
    d = -1.23;
    Console.WriteLine("{0:C6}", d); // ($1.230000)
    Console.WriteLine("{0:E6}", d); // -1.230000E+000
    Console.WriteLine("{0:G6}", d); // -1.23
    Console.WriteLine("{0:N6}", d); // -1.230000
    d = 0;
    Console.WriteLine("{0:C6}", d); // $0.000000
```

```
    Console.WriteLine("{0:E6}", d); // 0.000000E+000
    Console.WriteLine("{0:G6}", d); // 0
    Console.WriteLine("{0:N6}", d); // 0.000000
  }
}
```

Picture Format Specifiers

Table C-2 lists the valid picture format specifiers supported by the `Format` method on the predefined numeric types (see the documentation for `System.IFormattable` in the .NET SDK).

Table C-2. Picture Format Specifiers

Specifier	String Result
0	Zero placeholder
#	Digit placeholder
.	Decimal point
,	Group separator or multiplier
%	Percent notation
E+0, E-0 e+0, e-0	Exponent notation
\	Literal character quote
'xx' "xx"	Literal string quote
;	Section separator

Here's an example using picture-format specifiers on some `int` values:

```
using System;
class TestIntegerCustomFormats {
  static void Main() {
    int i = 123;
    Console.WriteLine("{0:#0}", i);                  // 123
    Console.WriteLine("{0:#0;(#0)}", i);             // 123
    Console.WriteLine("{0:#0;(#0);<zero>}", i); // 123
    Console.WriteLine("{0:#%}", i);                  // 12300%
    i = -123;
    Console.WriteLine("{0:#0}", i);                  // -123
    Console.WriteLine("{0:#0;(#0)}", i);             // (123)
    Console.WriteLine("{0:#0;(#0);<zero>}", i); // (123)
    Console.WriteLine("{0:#%}", i);                  // -12300%
    i = 0;
    Console.WriteLine("{0:#0}", i);                  // 0
    Console.WriteLine("{0:#0;(#0)}", i);             // 0
    Console.WriteLine("{0:#0;(#0);<zero>}", i); // <zero>
    Console.WriteLine("{0:#%}", i);                  // %
  }
}
```

The following is an example that uses these picture format specifiers on a variety of `double` values:

```
using System;
class TestDoubleCustomFormats {
  static void Main() {
    double d = 1.23;
    Console.WriteLine("{0:#.000E+00}", d);        // 1.230E+00
    Console.WriteLine(
      "{0:#.000E+00;(#.000E+00)}", d);            // 1.230E+00
    Console.WriteLine(
      "{0:#.000E+00;(#.000E+00);<zero>}", d);     // 1.230E+00
    Console.WriteLine("{0:#%}", d);               // 123%
    d = -1.23;
    Console.WriteLine("{0:#.000E+00}", d);        // -1.230E+00
    Console.WriteLine(
      "{0:#.000E+00;(#.000E+00)}", d);            // (1.230E+00)
    Console.WriteLine(
      "{0:#.000E+00;(#.000E+00);<zero>}", d);     // (1.230E+00)
    Console.WriteLine("{0:#%}", d);               // -123%
    d = 0;
    Console.WriteLine("{0:#.000E+00}", d);        // 0.000E-01
    Console.WriteLine(
      "{0:#.000E+00;(#.000E+00)}", d);            // 0.000E-01
    Console.WriteLine(
      "{0:#.000E+00;(#.000E+00);<zero>}", d);     // <zero>
    Console.WriteLine("{0:#%}", d);               // %
  }
}
```

DateTime Format Specifiers

Table C-3 lists the valid format specifiers supported by the Format method on the DateTime type (see System.IFormattable).

Table C-3. DateTime Format Specifiers

Specifier	String Result
D	MM/dd/yyyy
d	dddd, MMMM dd, yyyy
f	dddd, MMMM dd, yyyy HH:mm
F	dddd, MMMM dd, yyyy HH:mm:ss
g	MM/dd/yyyy HH:mm
G	MM/dd/yyyy HH:mm:ss
m, M	MMMM dd
r, R	Ddd, dd MMM yyyy HH':'mm':'ss 'GMT'
s	yyyy-MM-dd HH:mm:ss
S	yyyy-MM-dd HH:mm:ss GMT
t	HH:mm
T	HH:mm:ss
u	yyyy-MM-dd HH:mm:ss

Table C-3. DateTime Format Specifiers (continued)

Specifier	String Result
U	dddd, MMMM dd, yyyy HH:mm:ss
y, Y	MMMM, yyyy

Here's an example that uses these custom format specifiers on a DateTime value:

```
using System;
class TestDateTimeFormats {
  static void Main() {
    DateTime dt = new DateTime(2000, 10, 11, 15, 32, 14);
    // Prints "2000-10-11T15:32:14"
    Console.WriteLine(dt.ToString());
    // Prints "Wednesday, October 11, 2000"
    Console.WriteLine("{0}", dt);
    // Prints "10/11/2000"
    Console.WriteLine("{0:d}", dt);
    // Prints "Wednesday, October 11, 2000"
    Console.WriteLine("{0:D}", dt);
    // Prints "Wednesday, October 11, 2000 3:32 PM"
    Console.WriteLine("{0:f}", dt);
    // Prints "Wednesday, October 11, 2000 3:32:14 PM"
    Console.WriteLine("{0:F}", dt);
    // Prints "10/11/2000 3:32 PM"
    Console.WriteLine("{0:g}", dt);
    // Prints "10/11/2000 3:32:14 PM"
    Console.WriteLine("{0:G}", dt);
    // Prints "October 11"
    Console.WriteLine("{0:m}", dt);
    // Prints "October 11"
    Console.WriteLine("{0:M}", dt);
    // Prints "Wed, 11 Oct 2000 22:32:14 GMT"
    Console.WriteLine("{0:r}", dt);
    // Prints "Wed, 11 Oct 2000 22:32:14 GMT"
    Console.WriteLine("{0:R}", dt);
    // Prints "3:32 PM"
    Console.WriteLine("{0:t}", dt);
    // Prints "3:32:14 PM"
    Console.WriteLine("{0:T}", dt);
    // Prints "2000-10-11 22:32:14Z"
    Console.WriteLine("{0:u}", dt);
    // Prints "Wednesday, October 11, 2000 10:32:14 PM"
    Console.WriteLine("{0:U}", dt);
    // Prints "October, 2000"
    Console.WriteLine("{0:y}", dt);
    // Prints "October, 2000"
    Console.WriteLine("{0:Y}", dt);
    // Prints "Wednesday the 11 day of October in the year 2000"
    Console.WriteLine(
      "{0:dddd 'the' d 'day of' MMMM 'in the year' yyyy}", dt);
  }
}
```

D

Data Marshaling

When calling between the runtime environment and existing COM interfaces, the CLR performs automatic data marshaling for CLR types into compatible COM types.

Table D-1 describes the C# to COM default data type mapping.

Table D-1. C# Type to COM Type Mapping

C# Type	COM Type
bool	VARIANT_BOOL
char	unsigned short
sbyte	Char
byte	Unsigned char
short	Short
ushort	Unsigned short
int	Int
uint	Unsigned int
long	Hyper
ulong	Unsigned hyper
float	Single
double	Double
decimal	DECIMAL
object	VARIANT
string	BSTR
System.DateTime	DATE[a]
System.Guid	GUID

Table D-1. C# Type to COM Type Mapping (continued)

C# Type	COM Type
System.Currency	CURRENCY
1-dimensional arrays	SAFEARRAY
Value types	Equivalently named struct
enum	Equivalently named enum
interface	Equivalently named interface
class	Equivalently named CoClass

[a] COM dates are less precise, causing comparison problems.

Table D-2 shows the mapping of the C# modifiers to their equivalent COM interface attributes.

Table D-2. C# Modifier/COM Attribute Mapping

C# Modifier	COM Attribute
<no modifier>	[in]
out	[out]
ref	[in, out]
<return value>	[out, retval]

E

Working with
Assemblies

This appendix describes a number of useful techniques for working with
assemblies. Among the topics covered are how to create modules, how to
manage the global assembly cache, how to make assemblies shareable,
and how to use the *nmake* utility to automate your builds.

Building Shareable Assemblies

For most applications you build components that are either standalone
assembly EXEs or DLLs. If you want to build shareable components that
are shared across multiple applications, you need to give your assembly a
strong name (using the *sn* utility) and install it into the shared assembly
(using the *al* utility).

Building Modules

The *al* utility doesn't rebuild assemblies from other assemblies, so you
need to compile your C# files as modules, using the flag (*/target:module*).
Here's an example:

```
csc /target:module a.cs
```

Linking Modules to Assemblies

Once your modules are built, you can create a single shared assembly
with the *al* (*alink*) utility. You specify the name of the new assembly and
the source modules. Here's an example:

```
al /out:c.dll a.dll b.dll
```

Building with Your New Assemblies

You can now create applications with the new assembly by referencing it on the compiler command line. Example:

```
csc /r:c.dll d.cs
```

Note that in order to use classes within the namespaces contained in the *c.dll* assembly of the preceding example, you need to specify the using keyword to reference the namespace.

Sharing Assemblies

To share assemblies across multiple applications where the assembly itself doesn't reside in the same directory, you need to install it into the assembly cache. To install an assembly into the cache, it must be signed with a strong name.

The sequence:

1. You must generate a key file. Example:

```
sn -k key.snk
```

2. Then build an assembly that is signed with the strong name:

```
al /out:e.dll /keyfile:key.snk a.dll b.dll
```

3. Once your assembly is signed, you can install it in the global assembly cache.

Note that installing an assembly to the shared cache doesn't copy it to anywhere, so when specifying the reference on compilations, you need to specify the assembly file location for the compiler:

```
csc /r:..\e.dll f.cs
```

Managing the Global Assembly Cache

There are two ways to work with the assembly cache. One is the Windows Explorer, which has a shell extension that displays the cache and allows you to manipulate the entries. If you explore the *c:\winnt\assembly* directory, you can display the current cache:

```
start c:\winnt\assembly
```

Alternately you can use the *gacutil* utility, which allows you to install, uninstall, and list the contents of the global assembly cache. The following:

```
gacutil /i e.dll
```

installs *e.dll*.

This example:

```
gacutil /u e
```

uninstalls all assemblies with the name **e**.

This example:

```
gacutil /u e,ver=0.0.0.0
```

uninstalls only the assembly **e** that matches the version number.

Using nmake

You can use *nmake* to automate many tasks that build assemblies and modules. Here's an example that shows many of the previous command lines, in a cohesive manner. Particular *nmake* features to note are the use of the .SUFFIXES keyword to add a definition for the *.cs* file extension and the use of the response file with the C# compiler, for when more source-file names are being supplied that can be listed on the command line.

```
REF=/r:c.dll
DEBUG=/debug
.SUFFIXES: .exe .dll .cs
.cs.dll:
    csc /t:module $*.cs
.cs.exe:
    csc $(DEBUG) $(REF) @<<big.tmp
$*.cs $(SRCLIST)
<<
all : d.exe f.exe
d.exe : d.cs c.dll
c.dll : a.dll b.dll
    al /out:c.dll a.dll b.dll
b.dll : b.cs
a.dll : a.cs
key.snk :
    sn -k $*.snk
e.dll : a.dll b.dll key.snk
    al /out:$*.dll /keyfile:key.snk a.dll b.dll
    al /i:$*.dll
f.exe : f.cs e.dll
    csc $(DEBUG) /r:.\e.dll f.cs
clean:
    del a.dll b.dll c.dll d.exe /q
```

F

Namespaces and Assemblies

This appendix allows you to look up a namespace and determine what assemblies export that namespace. This information is helpful when constructing the appropriate `/reference:<file list>` command-line option for the C# compiler. Note that *mscorlib.dll* is implicitly referenced by the compiler unless the `/nostdlib` command-line option is used.

Namespace	DLLs
Accessibility	*Accessibility.dll*
IIEHost	*IEHost.dll, IIEHost.dll*
Microsoft.ASPXCompiler	*Microsoft.ASPXCompiler.dll*
Microsoft.ComServices	*Microsoft.ComServices.dll*
Microsoft.CSharp	*cscompmgd.dll*
Microsoft.JScript	*Microsoft.JScript.dll*
Microsoft.VisualBasic	*Microsoft.VisualBasic.dll*
Microsoft.VisualBasic. Compatibility.VB6	*Microsoft.VisualBasic.dll, Microsoft.VisualBasic.Compatibility.dll*
Microsoft.VisualBasic.Helpers	*Microsoft.VisualBasic.dll*
Microsoft.VisualC	*Microsoft.VisualC.dll*
Microsoft.Vsa	*Microsoft.Vsa.dll*
Microsoft.Win32	*mscorlib.dll*
Microsoft.Win32.Interop	*Microsoft.Win32.Interop.dll*
Microsoft.Win32.Interop. Trident	*Microsoft.Win32.Interop.dll*
System	*mscorlib.dll, System.Net.dll*
System.CodeDOM	*System.dll*

Namespace	DLLs
System.CodeDOM.Compiler	*System.dll*
System.Collections	*mscorlib.dll, System.dll*
System.Collections.Bases	*System.dll*
System.ComponentModel	*mscorlib.dll, System.dll*
System.ComponentModel.Design	*System.dll, System.ComponentModel.Design.dll*
System.Component-Model.Design.CodeModel	*System.dll*
System.ComponentModel.Interop	*System.dll*
System.Configuration	*System.Configuration.dll*
System.Configuration.Assemblies	*mscorlib.dll*
System.Configuration.Core	*System.Configuration.Objects.dll*
System.Configuration.Design	*System.Configuration.Design.dll*
System.Configuration.Install	*System.Configuration.Install.dll*
System.Configuration.Interceptors	*System.Configuration.dll*
System.Configuration.Internal	*System.Configuration.dll*
System.Configuration.Schema	*System.Configuration.dll, System.Configuration.Objects.dll*
System.Configuration.Web	*System.Configuration.Objects.dll*
System.Core	*System.dll*
System.Data	*System.Data.dll*
System.Data.ADO	*System.Data.dll*
System.Data.ADO.Interop	*System.Data.dll*
System.Data.CodeGen	*System.Data.dll*
System.Data.Design	*System.Data.Design.dll*
System.Data.Internal	*System.Data.dll*
System.Data.SQL	*System.Data.dll*
System.Data.SQLTypes	*System.Data.dll*
System.Diagnostics	*mscorlib.dll, System.dll, System.Diagnostics.dll*
System.Diagnostics.Design	*System.Diagnostics.dll, System.Diagnostics.Design.dll*
System.Diagnostics.SymbolStore	*mscorlib.dll*
System.DirectoryServices	*System.DirectoryServices.dll*
System.Drawing	*System.Drawing.dll*
System.Drawing.Design	*System.Drawing.dll, System.Drawing.Design.dll, System.WinForms.dll*

Namespace	DLLs
System.Drawing.Drawing2D	*System.Drawing.dll*
System.Drawing.Imaging	*System.Drawing.dll*
System.Drawing.Printing	*System.Drawing.dll*
System.Drawing.Text	*System.Drawing.dll*
System.Globalization	*mscorlib.dll*
System.IO	*mscorlib.dll, System.IO.dll*
System.IO.IsolatedStorage	*mscorlib.dll*
System.Management	*System.Management.dll*
System.Messaging	*System.Messaging.dll*
System.Messaging.Design	*System.Messaging.dll*
System.Net	*System.Net.dll*
System.Net.Sockets	*System.Net.dll*
System.Reflection	*mscorlib.dll*
System.Reflection.Emit	*mscorlib.dll*
System.Resources	*mscorlib.dll, System.dll, System.WinForms.dll*
System.Runtime.CompilerServices	*mscorlib.dll*
System.Runtime.CompilerServices.CSharp	*mscorlib.dll*
System.Runtime.InteropServices	*mscorlib.dll*
System.Runtime.InteropServices.CustomMarshalers	*CustomMarshalers.dll*
System.Runtime.InteropServices.Expando	*mscorlib.dll*
System.Runtime.Remoting	*mscorlib.dll*
System.Runtime.Remoting.Channels.Core	*System.Runtime.Remoting.dll*
System.Runtime.Remoting.Channels.HTTP	*System.Runtime.Remoting.dll*
System.Runtime.Remoting.Channels.SMTP	*System.Runtime.Remoting.dll*
System.Runtime.Remoting.Channels.TCP	*System.Runtime.Remoting.dll*
System.Runtime.Remoting.MetadataServices	*System.Runtime.Remoting.dll*
System.Runtime.Remoting.Services	*System.Runtime.Remoting.dll*
System.Runtime.Serialization	*mscorlib.dll*
System.Runtime.Serialization.Formatters	*mscorlib.dll*

Namespace	DLLs
System.Runtime.Serialization.Formatters.Binary	*mscorlib.dll*
System.Runtime.Serialization.Formatters.Soap	*System.Runtime.Serialization.Formatters.Soap.dll*
System.Security	*mscorlib.dll*
System.Security.Cryptography	*mscorlib.dll, System.Security.dll*
System.Security.Cryptography.X509Certificates	*mscorlib.dll*
System.Security.Cryptography.Xml	*System.Security.dll*
System.Security.Permissions	*mscorlib.dll*
System.Security.Policy	*mscorlib.dll*
System.Security.Principal	*mscorlib.dll*
System.ServiceProcess	*System.ServiceProcess.dll*
System.Text	*mscorlib.dll*
System.Text.RegularExpressions	*System.Text.RegularExpressions.dll*
System.Threading	*mscorlib.dll,System.dll*
System.Timers	*System.Timers.dll*
System.Timers.Design	*System.Timers.dll*
System.Web	*System.Web.dll*
System.Web.Caching	*System.Web.dll*
System.Web.Configuration	*System.Web.dll*
System.Web.Handlers	*System.Web.dll*
System.Web.Hosting	*System.Web.dll*
System.Web.Security	*System.Web.dll*
System.Web.Services	*System.Web.Services.dll*
System.Web.Services.Description	*System.Web.Services.dll*
System.Web.Services.Discovery	*System.Web.Services.dll*
System.Web.Services.Interop	*System.Web.Services.dll*
System.Web.Services.Protocols	*System.Web.Services.dll*
System.Web.SessionState	*System.Web.dll*
System.Web.UI	*System.Web.dll*
System.Web.UI.Design	*System.Web.UI.Design.dll*
System.Web.UI.Design.Util	*System.Web.UI.Design.dll*
System.Web.UI.Design.WebControls	*System.Web.UI.Design.dll*
System.Web.UI.Design.WebControls.ListControls	*System.Web.UI.Design.dll*

Namespace	DLLs
System.Web.UI.HtmlControls	*System.Web.dll*
System.Web.UI.WebControls	*System.Web.dll*
System.Web.UI.WebControls.Design	*System.Web.dll*
System.Web.Util	*System.Web.dll*
System.WinForms	*System.WinForms.dll*
System.WinForms.ComponentModel	*System.WinForms.dll*
System.WinForms.ComponentModel.COM2Interop	*System.WinForms.dll*
System.WinForms.Design	*System.WinForms.dll, System.WinForms.Design.dll*
System.WinForms.PropertyGridInternal	*System.WinForms.dll*
System.Xml	*System.Data.dll, System.XML.dll*
System.Xml.Serialization	*System.Xml.Serialization.dll*
System.Xml.Serialization.IO	*System.Xml.Serialization.dll*
System.Xml.Serialization.Schema	*System.Xml.Serialization.dll*
System.Xml.XPath	*System.XML.dll*
System.Xml.Xsl	*System.XML.dll*
WbemClient_v1	*wbemclient_v1.dll*
WbemUtilities_v1	*WbemUtilities_v1.dll*

Index

Symbols

Numbers

A

P

Q

R

X

About the Authors

Ben Albahari is cofounder of Genamics, a provider of tools for C# and J++ programmers, as well as software for DNA and protein sequence analysis. He is author of "A Comparative Overview of C#", a frequently cited comparison of C# with C/C++ and Java (*http://www.genamics.com/visualj++/csharp_comparative.htm*) that was recently named one of the top 10 .NET sites by DevX (*http://www.devx.com/dotnet/resources/vsresources-17.asp*). Ben is a resident of Perth, Australia, and in his spare time enjoys composing music on his computer. He can be reached at *ben@genamics.com*.

Peter Drayton is an independent consultant, helping early-stage companies define and build systems that take advantage of technologies such as .NET, SOAP, XML, and COM+. Peter is also an instructor for DevelopMentor, where he teaches Essential C#.NET. Originally from Cape Town, South Africa, Peter now lives in the San Francisco Bay Area with his wife, Julie. He spends his spare time researching .NET and tinkering with a small flotilla of computers cluttering up their apartment. He can be reached at *peter@razorsoft.com*.

Brad Merrill works as a software engineer in the .NET Framework Integration team at Microsoft. He previously worked as a software engineer at Digital Equipment Corporation and Sybase. His areas of expertise are in distributed systems, transaction processing, operating systems, and compiler technology. Brad lives in Redmond, Washington, and is an avid tournament chess player and bridge player. He can be reached at *zbrad@gte.net* or *http://www.cybercom.net/~zbrad*.

Colophon

Our look is the result of reader comments, our own experimentation, and feedback from distribution channels. Distinctive covers complement our distinctive approach to technical topics, breathing personality and life into potentially dry subjects.

The animal on the cover of *C# Essentials* is a star-nosed mole (*condylura cristata*). Like all moles, star-nosed moles live primarily in underground tunnels they dig, but they do surface to find food. A mole's rodent-like body is covered in short, waterproof gray fur, and it is about six to eight inches long. A notable feature is its long claws, which are perfect for digging its trenches and foraging for food. It has small ears and eyes, and sharp pointed teeth. A mole's eyesight and hearing are known to be terrible.

The star-nosed mole gets its name from the approximate 25 feelers on its nose that help it find food, primarily insects, worms, and small fish, as well as other small pond life. The star-nosed mole is the best swimmer in the mole family and can even dive to catch a fish. It prefers to live in wetlands but can be found in various areas of the Northeast United States and Southeast Canada.

Moles are mammals who nurse their young, and a female mole has one litter of three to six babies per year.

This particular type of mole is considered to be less of a household pest than its mole cousins because its mostly aquatic diet keeps it from rummaging around in backyards for food.

Mary Anne Weeks Mayo was the copyeditor and production editor for *C# Essentials*. Jane Ellin proofread the book. Nicole Arigo provided quality control. Matt Hutchinson provided production assistance. Joe Wizda wrote the index.

Ellie Volckhausen designed the cover of this book, based on a series design by Edie Freedman. The cover image is an original engraving from *The Illustrated Natural History* by J. G. Wood, published in 1865. Emma Colby produced the cover layout with QuarkXPress 4.1 using Adobe's ITC Garamond font.

David Futato and Melanie Wang designed the interior layout based on a series design by Nancy Priest. Anne-Marie Vaduva converted the files form MSWord to FrameMaker 5.5 using tools created by Mike Sierra. The text and heading fonts are ITC Garamond Light and Garamond Book. This colophon was written by Nicole Arigo.

Whenever possible, our books use a durable and flexible lay-flat binding. If the page count exceeds this binding's limit, perfect binding is used.

O'REILLY®

O'Reilly & Associates, Inc.
101 Morris Street
Sebastopol, CA 95472-9902
1-800-998-9938

Visit us online at:
www.oreilly.com
order@oreilly.com

O'REILLY WOULD LIKE TO HEAR FROM YOU

Which book did this card come from?

_____

Where did you buy this book?
- ❏ Bookstore   ❏ Computer Store
- ❏ Direct from O'Reilly   ❏ Class/seminar
- ❏ Bundled with hardware/software
- ❏ Other _____

What operating system do you use?
- ❏ UNIX   ❏ Macintosh
- ❏ Windows NT   ❏ PC(Windows/DOS)
- ❏ Other _____

What is your job description?
- ❏ System Administrator   ❏ Programmer
- ❏ Network Administrator ❏ Educator/Teacher
- ❏ Web Developer
- ❏ Other _____

> ❏ Please send me O'Reilly's catalog, containing
> a complete listing of O'Reilly books and
> software.

Name _____ Company/Organization _____

Address _____

City _____ State _____ Zip/Postal Code _____ Country _____

Telephone _____ Internet or other email address (specify network)

Nineteenth century wood engraving
of a bear from the O'Reilly &
Associates Nutshell Handbook®
Using & Managing UUCP.

BUSINESS REPLY MAIL
FIRST CLASS MAIL   PERMIT NO. 80   SEBASTOPOL, CA

Postage will be paid by addressee

O'Reilly & Associates, Inc.
101 Morris Street
Sebastopol, CA 95472-9902